National Wetlands Inventory

SEPTEMBER 1985

WETLANDS OF DELAWARE

U.S. Department of the Interior

State of Delaware

Fish and Wildlife Service

Department of Natural Resources and Environmental Control

WETLANDS OF DELAWARE

Ralph W. Tiner, Jr.
Regional Wetland Coordinator
Habitat Resources
U.S. Fish and Wildlife Service
Region 5
Newton Corner, MA 02158

SEPTEMBER 1985

Project Officer
David L. Hardin
Department of Natural Resources and Environmental Control
Wetlands Section
State of Delaware
89 Kings Highway
Dover, DE 19903

Cooperative Publication

U.S. Fish and Wildlife Service
Region 5
Habitat Resources
One Gateway Center
Newton Corner, MA 02158

Delaware Department of Natural
Resources and Environmental
Control
Division of Environmental Control
89 Kings Highway
Dover, DE 19903

This report should be cited as follows:

Tiner, R.W., Jr. 1985. Wetlands of Delaware. U.S. Fish and Wildlife Service, National Wetlands Inventory, Newton Corner, MA and Delaware Department of Natural Resources and Environmental Control, Wetlands Section, Dover, DE. Cooperative Publication. 77 pp.

Acknowledgements

Many individuals have contributed to the successful completion of the wetlands inventory in Delaware and to the preparation of this report. The Delaware Department of Natural Resources and Environmental Control, Wetlands Section contributed funds for wetland mapping and database construction and printed this report. David Hardin served as project officer for this work and offered invaluable assistance throughout the project, especially in coordinating technical review of the draft report and during field investigations. The U.S. Army Corps of Engineers, Philadelphia District also provided funds for map production.

William Zinni and Anthony Davis performed wetland photo interpretation and quality control of draft maps, and reviewed portions of this report. Their work serves as the foundation for this report. John Organ provided quality control of interpreted photographs. The Service's National Wetlands Inventory Group in St. Petersburg, Florida provided technical support for producing the wetland maps and for creating the Delaware wetland database. In particular, John Montanari, Ross Pywell, Robin Gebhard, and Susan Hazellief provided major support.

The following persons reviewed the draft manuscript and provided additional information: Dr. John Carey (DNREC), Inez Connor (FWS), Dr. Franklin Daiber (University of Delaware), Richard Dyer (FWS), Tony Florio (DNREC), Dick Hall (SCS), Dr. Glenn Kinser (FWS), Charles Lesser (DNREC), Dr. Blake Parker (FWS), Ron Vickers (DNREC), Dr. Bill Wilen (FWS), and Bob Zepp (FWS).

The work of the individuals who typed portions of this report and its earlier draft is acknowledged: Lynne Ricci (draft manuscript), Alicia Bruneau (tables), Priscilla Arsenault (final manuscript), and Rachel Caliendo (final manuscript). Graphic support was provided by Debra McGeever and the enclosed figure showing the distribution of Delaware's wetlands was prepared by Kelly Drake and Fred Seavey.

Cover photo credits: Martin (wood duck), Tiner (estuarine emergent wetland), Tiner (swamp milkweed) Zinni (palustrine forested wetland), Zinni (wetland with skunk cabbage), and Fitzharris (great blue heron).

Table of Contents

List of Figures

List of Tables

List of Plates

CHAPTER 1.

Introduction

Wet habitats generally occurring between uplands and deepwater areas are considered wetlands. They are commonly referred to by a host of terms based on their location and characteristics, such as salt marsh, tidal marsh, wet meadow, cedar swamp, and hardwood swamp. These areas are important natural resources with numerous values, e.g., fish and wildlife habitat, flood protection, erosion control, and water quality maintenance.

The Fish and Wildlife Service (Service) has always recognized the importance of wetlands to waterfowl, other migratory birds and wildlife. The Service's responsibility for protecting these habitats comes largely from international treaties concerning migratory birds and from the Fish and Wildlife Coordination Act. The Service has been active in protecting these resources through various programs. The Service's National Wildlife Refuge System was established to preserve and enhance migratory bird habitat in strategic locations across the country. More than 10 million ducks breed annually in U.S. wetlands and millions more overwinter here. The Service also reviews Federal projects and applications for Federal permit that involve wetland alteration.

Since the 1950's, the Service has been particularly concerned about wetland losses and their impact on fish and wildlife populations. In 1954, the Service conducted its first nationwide wetlands inventory which focused on important waterfowl wetlands. This survey was performed to provide information for considering fish and wildlife impacts in land-use decisions. The results of this inventory were published in a well known Service report entitled **Wetlands of the United States**, commonly referred to as Circular 39 (Shaw and Fredine 1956).

Since this survey, wetlands have undergone many changes, both natural and human-induced. The conversion of wetlands for agriculture, residential and industrial developments and other uses has continued. During the 1960's, the general public in many states became more aware of wetland values and concerned about wetland losses. They began to realize that wetlands provided significant public benefits besides fish and wildlife habitat, especially flood protection and water quality maintenance. Prior to this time, wetlands were regarded by most people as wastelands, whose best use could only be attained by alteration, e.g., draining for agriculture, dredging and filling for industrial and housing developments and filling with sanitary landfill. Scientific studies demonstrating wetland values, especially for coastal marshes, were instrumental in increasing public awareness of wetland benefits and stimulating concern for wetland protection. Consequently, several states passed laws to protect coastal wetlands, including Massachusetts (1963), Rhode Island (1965), Connecticut (1969), New Jersey (1970), Maryland (1970), Georgia (1970), New York (1972) and Delaware (1973). Four of these states subsequently adopted inland or nontidal wetland protection legislation, i.e., Massachusetts, Rhode Island, Connecticut and New York. Most of the other states in the Nation with coastal wetlands followed the lead of these northeastern states and enacted laws to protect or regulate uses of coastal wetlands. During the early 1970's, the Federal government also assumed greater responsibility for wetlands through Section 404 of the Federal Water Pollution Control Act of 1972 (later amended as the Clean Water Act of 1977) and by strengthening wetland protection under Section 10 of the River and Harbor Act of 1899. Federal permits are now required for many types of construction in many wetlands, although normal agricultural and forestry activities are exempt.

With increased public interest in wetlands and strengthened government regulation, the Service considered how it could contribute to this resource management effort, since it has prime responsibility for protection and management of the Nation's fish and wildlife and their habitats. The Service still recognized the need for sound ecological information to make decisions regarding policy, planning, and management of the country's wetland resources and established the National Wetlands Inventory Project (NWI) in 1974 to fulfill this need. The NWI aims to generate scientific information on the characteristics and extent of the Nation's wetlands. The purpose of this information is to foster wise use of U.S. wetlands and to provide data for making quick and accurate resource decisions.

Two very different kinds of information are needed: (1) detailed maps and (2) status and trends reports. First, detailed wetland maps are needed for impact assessment of site-specific projects. These maps serve a purpose similar to the Soil Conservation Service's soil survey maps, the National Oceanic and Atmospheric Administration's coastal and geodetic survey maps, and the Geological Survey's topographic maps. Detailed wetland maps are used by local, state and Federal agencies as well as by private industry and organizations for many purposes, including watershed management plans, environmental impact assessments, permit reviews, facility and corridor siting, oil spill contingency plans, natural resource inventories, wildlife surveys and other uses. To date, wetland maps have been prepared for 40% of the lower 48 states, 10% of Alaska, and all of Hawaii. Secondly, national estimates of the current status and recent losses and gains of wetlands are needed in order to provide improved information for reviewing the effectiveness of existing Federal programs and policies, for identifying national or regional problems and for general public awareness. Technical and popular reports about these trends have been recently published (Frayer, *et al.* 1983; Tiner 1984).

Need for a Wetlands Inventory in Delaware

A wetlands inventory was needed for Delaware for several reasons: (1) no detailed information existed on the distribution and extent of Delaware's wetlands and deepwater habitats, (2) increasing development pressure threatens the remaining inland wetlands, and (3) many inland wetlands were still not adequately protected by state or Federal law. Although extensive mapping of coastal wetlands had been completed by the state, no comparable maps existed for inland wetlands. Also, changes in coastal wetlands have occurred since the state's maps were prepared in the early 1970's. While coastal wetlands were protected through the Wetlands Act of 1973, development pressures on inland wetlands have continued. Although the Federal Clean Water Act of 1977 provided some control over wetland uses involving deposition of fill, many inland wetlands were still relatively unprotected. Thus, in 1982, the Service initiated a wetlands inventory in Delaware to provide government administrators, private industry and others with improved information for project planning and impact evaluation and for making land-use decisions. This inventory would identify the current status of Delaware's wetlands and serve as the base from which future changes can be determined.

Description of the Study Area

Delaware is one of 13 northeastern states within the Service's Region 5. Delaware's landscape is dominated by the Coastal Plain, with only 6% of the state represented by the Piedmont (Figure 1). The nearly level Coastal Plain is contrasted by the rolling Piedmont which occupies the northern tip of the state.

The climate for each of Delaware's counties has been described in the U.S.D.A. Soil Conservation Service's

county soil survey reports (Ireland and Matthews 1974; Matthews and Lavoie 1970; Matthews and Ireland 1971). Delaware has a temperate humid continental climate, modified by its proximity to the Atlantic Ocean. Annual precipitation averages about 45 inches, with generally uniform monthly distribution, but maximum rainfall in August. Thunderstorms occur mostly from May through August. Snowfall is heaviest in New Castle County averaging 21.4 inches at Wilmington compared to 16 inches in Sussex County. Average temperatures range from a maximum around 87 °F in July to a minimum in the low 20's °F in late January and early February. The last freeze occurs from late March to early May, while the first frost occurs from early October to mid-November.

Purpose and Organization of this Report

The purpose of this publication is to report the findings of the Service's wetlands inventory of Delaware - the second state completed by the National Wetlands Inventory. The following chapters will include discussions of wetland concept and classification (Chapter 2), inventory techniques and results (Chapter 3), wetland hydrology (Chapter 4), hydric soils (Chapter 5), wetland vegetation and plant communities (Chapter 6), wetland values (Chapter 7), wetland trends (Chapter 8), and wetland protection (Chapter 9). The appendix contains a list of vascular plants associated with Delaware's wetlands. Scientific names of plants follow the **National List of Scientific Plant Names** (U.S.D.A. Soil Conservation Service 1982). A figure showing the general distribution of Delaware's wetlands and deepwater habitats is provided as an enclosure at the back of this report.

References

Frayer, W.E., T.J. Monahan, D.C. Bowden, and F.A. Graybill. 1983. Status and Trends of Wetlands and Deepwater Habitats in the Conterminous United States, 1950's to 1970's. Dept. of Forest and Wood Sciences, Colorado State University, Ft. Collins. 32 pp.

Ireland, W., Jr. and E.D. Matthews. 1974. Soil Survey of Sussex County, Delaware. U.S.D.A. Soil Conservation Service. 74 pp. and maps.

Matthews, E.D. and O.L. Lavoie. 1970. Soil Survey of New Castle County, Delaware. U.S.D.A. Soil Conservation Service. 97 pp. and maps.

Matthews, E.D. and W. Ireland, Jr. 1971. Soil Survey of Kent County, Delaware. U.S.D.A. Soil Conservation Service. 66 pp. and maps.

Shaw, S.P. and C.G. Fredine. 1956. Wetlands of the United States. Their Extent and Their Value to Waterfowl and Other Wildlife. U.S. Fish and Wildlife Service. Circular 39. 67 pp.

Tiner, R.W., Jr. 1984. Wetlands of the United States: Current Status and Recent Trends. U.S. Fish and Wildlife Service, National Wetlands Inventory, Washington, DC. 59 pp.

U.S.D.A. Soil Conservation Service. 1982. National List of Scientific Plant Names. Vol. 1. List of Plant Names. SCS-TP-159 416 pp.

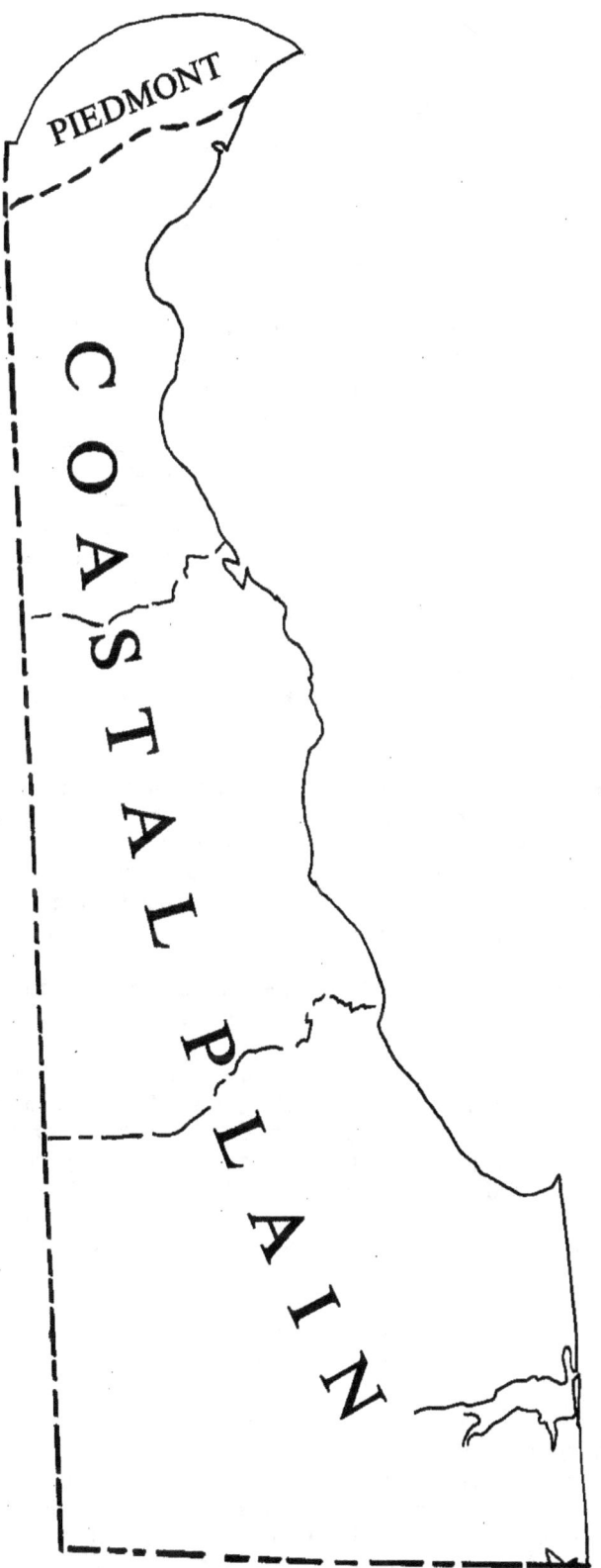

Figure 1. Physiographic regions of Delaware.

CHAPTER 2.

U.S. Fish and Wildlife Service's Wetland Definition and Classification System

Introduction

To begin inventorying the Nation's wetlands, the Service needed a definition of wetland and a classification system to identify various wetland types. The Service, therefore, examined recent wetland inventories throughout the country to learn how others defined and classified wetlands. The results of this examination were published as **Existing State and Local Wetlands Surveys (1965-1975)** (U.S. Fish and Wildlife Service 1976). More than 50 wetland classification schemes were identified. Of those, only one classification - the Martin, et al. system (1953) - was nationally based, while all others were regionally focused. In January 1975, the Service brought together 14 authors of regional wetland classifications and other prominent wetland scientists to help decide if any existing classification could be used or modified for the national inventory or if a new system was needed. They recommended that the Service attempt to develop a new national wetland classification. In July 1975, the Service sponsored the National Wetland Classification and Inventory Workshop, where more than 150 wetland scientists and mapping experts met to review a preliminary draft of the new wetland classification system. The consensus was that the system should be hierarchial in nature and built around the concept of ecosystems (Sather 1976).

Four key objectives for the new system were established: (1) to develop ecologically similar habitat units, (2) to arrange these units in a system that would facilitate resource management decisions, (3) to furnish units for inventory and mapping, and (4) to provide uniformity in concept and terminology throughout the country (Cowardin, et al. 1979).

The Service's wetland classification system was developed by a four member team, i.e., Dr. Lewis M. Cowardin (U.S. Fish and Wildlife Service), Virginia Carter (U.S. Geological Survey), Dr. Francis C. Golet (University of Rhode Island) and Dr. Edward T. LaRoe (National Oceanic and Atmospheric Administration), with assistance from numerous Federal and state agencies, university scientists, and other interested individuals. The classification system went through three major drafts and extensive field testing prior to its publication as **Classification of Wetlands and Deepwater Habitats of the United States** (Cowardin, et al.

1979). Since its publication, the Service's classification system has been widely used by Federal, state, and local agencies, university scientists, and private industry and non-profit organizations for identifying and classifying wetlands. At the First International Wetlands Conference in New Delhi, India, scientists from around the world adopted the Service's wetland definition as an international standard and recommended testing the applicability of the classification system in other areas, especially in the tropics and subtropics (Gopal, et al. 1982). Thus, the system appears to be moving quickly towards its goal of providing uniformity in wetland concept and terminology.

The Service's Definition of Wetland

Conceptually, wetlands lie between the better drained, rarely flooded uplands and the permanently flooded deep waters of lakes, rivers and coastal embayments (Figure 2). Wetlands generally include the variety of marshes, bogs, swamps, and bottomland forests that occur throughout the country. They usually lie in upland depressions or along rivers, lakes and coastal waters where they are subject to periodic flooding. Some wetlands, however, occur on slopes where they are associated with ground-water seepage areas. To accurately inventory this resource, the Service had to determine where along this natural wetness continuum wetland ends and upland begins. While many wetlands lie in distinct depressions or basins that are readily observable, the wetland-upland boundary is not always that easy to identify. This is especially true in the interior of Delaware where many wetlands occur in almost imperceptably shallow depressions, covering vast acreages with just a slight change in elevation. In these areas, only a skilled wetland ecologist or other specialist can accurately identify the wetland boundary. To help ensure accurate and consistent wetland determination, an ecologically based definition was constructed by the Service.

Wetlands were historically defined by scientists working in specialized fields, such as botany or hydrology. A botanical definition would focus on the plants adapted to flooding and/or saturated soil conditions, while a hydrologist's definition would emphasize fluctuations in the position of the water table

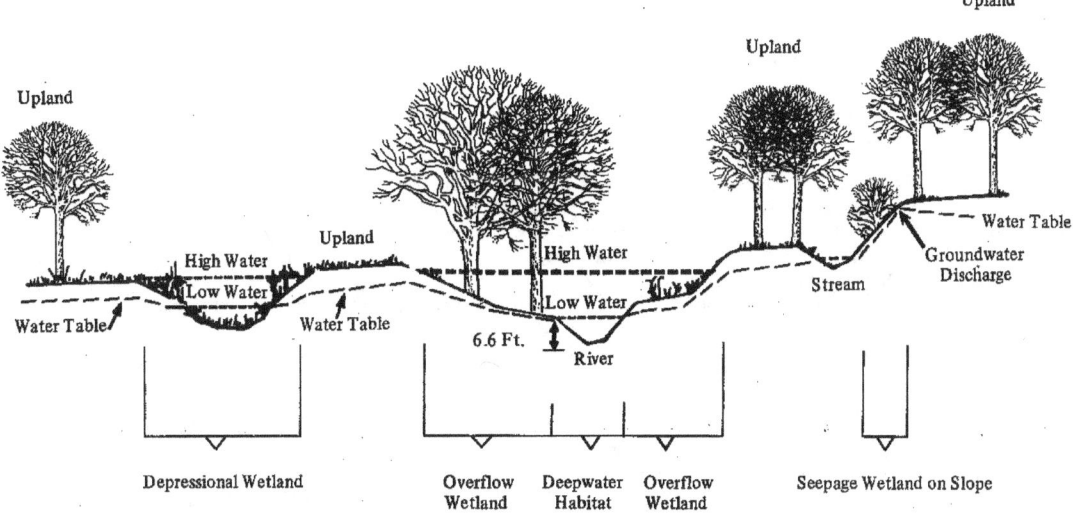

Figure 2. Schematic diagram showing wetlands, deepwater habitats, and uplands on the landscape. Note differences in wetlands due to hydrology and topographic position.

relative to the ground surface over time. A more complete definition of wetland involves a multi-disciplinary approach. The Service has taken this approach in developing its wetland definition and classification system.

In developing a multi-disciplinary definition of wetland, the Service first acknowledged that "There is no single, correct, indisputable, ecologically sound definition for wetlands, primarily because of the diversity of wetlands and because the demarcation between dry and wet environments lies along a continuum" (Cowardin, *et al.* 1979). After all, a wealth of wetland definitions grew out of different needs for defining wetlands among various groups or organizations, e.g., wetland regulators, waterfowl managers, hydrologists, flood control engineers and water quality experts. The Service has not attempted to legally define wetland, since each state or Federal regulatory agency has defined wetland somewhat differently to suit its administrative purposes (Table 1). Therefore, according to existing wetland laws, a wetland is whatever the law says it is. The Service needed a definition that would allow accurate identification and delineation of the Nation's wetlands for resource management purposes.

The Service specifically defines wetlands as follows: *"Wetlands are lands transitional between terrestrial and aquatic systems where the water table is usually at or near the surface or the land is covered by shallow water. For purposes of this classification wetlands must have one or more of the following three attributes: 1) at least periodically, the land supports predominantly hydrophytes; 2) the substrate is predominantly undrained hydric soil; and 3) the substrate is nonsoil and is*

saturated with water or covered by shallow water at some time during the growing season of each year." (Cowardin, *et al.* 1979).

In defining wetlands from an ecological standpoint, the Service emphasizes three key attributes of wetlands: (1) hydrology - the degree of flooding or soil saturation, (2) wetland vegetation (hydrophytes), and (3) hydric soils. All areas considered wetland must have enough water at some time during the growing season to stress plants and animals not adapted for life in water or saturated soils. Most wetlands have hydrophytes and hydric soils present. The Service has prepared a preliminary list of wetland plants and the Soil Conservation Service has developed a list of hydric soils to help identify wetland.

Particular attention should be paid to the reference to flooding or soil saturation during the growing season in the Service's wetland definition. When soils are covered by water or saturated to the surface, free oxygen is not available to plant roots. During the growing season, most plant roots must have access to free oxygen for respiration and growth; flooding at this time would have serious implications for the growth and survival of most plants. In a wetland situation, plants must be adapted to cope with these stressful conditions. If, however, flooding only occurs in winter when the plants are dormant, there is little or no effect on them.

Wetlands typically fall within one of the following five categories: (1) areas with both hydrophytes and hydric soils (e.g., marshes, swamps and bogs), (2) areas without hydrophytes, but with hydric soils (e.g., tidal flats), (3) areas with hydrophytes but with non-hydric

Table 1. Definitions of "wetland" according to selected Federal agencies and state statutes.

Organization (Reference)	Wetland Definition	Comments
U.S. Fish and Wildlife Service (Cowardin, *et al.* 1979)	"Wetlands are lands transitional between terrestrial and aquatic systems where the water table is usually at or near the surface or the land is covered by shallow water. For purposes of this classification wetlands must have one or more of the following three attributes: (1) at least periodically, the land supports predominantly hydrophytes; (2) the substrate is predominantly undrained hydric soil; and (3) the substrate is nonsoil and is saturated with water or covered by shallow water at some time during the growing season of each year."	This is the official Fish and Wildlife Service definition and is being used for conducting an inventory of the Nation's wetlands. It replaces the Circular 39 definition which is also outlined in this table. It emphasizes flooding and/or soil saturation, hydric soils and vegetation. Shallow lakes and ponds are included as wetland. Comprehensive lists of wetland plants and soils are available to further clarify this definition.
U.S. Fish and Wildlife Service and U.S.D.A Soil Conservation Service (Shaw and Fredine 1956; commonly referred to as "Circular 39")	Wetlands are "lowlands covered with shallow and sometimes temporary or intermittent waters." They include marshes, swamps, bogs, wet meadows, potholes, sloughs, river overflow lands, and shallow lakes and ponds.	Former Fish and Wildlife Service definition. Although this definition is generally weak, 20 individual wetland types were described in terms of water permanence and depth, salinity and vegetation. Wetland definition includes shallow lakes and ponds, but not permanent waters of streams, reservoirs, and deep lakes. This is the official definition of the Soil Conservation Service.
U.S. Army Corps of Engineers (Federal Register, July 19, 1977)	Wetlands are "those areas that are inundated or saturated by surface or ground water at a frequency and duration sufficient to support, and that under normal circumstances do support, a prevalence of vegetation typically adapted for life in saturated soil conditions. Wetlands generally include swamps, marshes, bogs and similar areas."	Regulatory definition in response to Section 404 of the Clean Water Act of 1977. Excludes similar areas lacking vegetation, such as tidal flats, and does not define lakes, ponds and rivers as wetland.
State of Delaware (Wetlands Act of 1973)	Wetlands are "those lands above the mean low water elevation including any bank, marsh, swamp, meadow, flat or other low land subject to tidal action in the State of Delaware, along the Delaware Bay and Delaware River, Indian River Bay, Rehoboth Bay, Little and Big Assawoman Bays, the coastal inland waterways, or along any inlet, estuary or tributary waterway or any portion thereof, including those areas which are now or in this century have been connected to tidal waters, whose surface is at or below an elevation of two feet above local mean high water, and upon which may grow or is capable of growing any but not necessarily all of the following plants:" (lists 29 plants) "and those lands not currently used for agricultural purposes containing four hundred (400) acres or more of contiguous non-tidal swamp, bog, muck, or marsh exclusive of narrow stream valleys where fresh water stands most, if not all, of the time due to high water table, which contribute significantly to ground water recharge, and which would require intensive artificial drainage using equipment such as pumping stations, drain fields or ditches for the production of agricultural crops."	State regulatory definition. Emphasizes coastal wetlands, but also includes contiguous non-tidal wetlands meeting certain criteria.

soils (e.g., margins of impoundments where hydrophytes have colonized non-hydric but now flooded soils), (4) areas without soils but with hydrophytes (e.g., seaweed-covered rocky shores), and (5) periodically flooded areas without soil and without hydrophytes (e.g., gravel beaches). Completely drained hydric soils that are no longer capable of supporting hydrophytes due to a change in water regime are not considered wetland. Areas with completely drained hydric soils are, however, good indicators of historic wetlands, which may be suitable for restoration through mitigation projects.

It is important to mention that the Service does not generally include permanently flooded deep water areas as wetland, although shallow waters are classified as wetland. Instead, these deeper water bodies are defined as deepwater habitats, since water and not air is the principal medium in which dominant organisms live. Along the coast in tidal areas, the deepwater habitat begins at the extreme spring low tide level. In nontidal freshwater areas, however, this habitat starts at a depth of 6.6 feet (2m) because the shallow water areas are often vegetated with emergent wetland plants.

The Service's Wetland Classification System

The following section represents a simplified overview of the Service's wetland classification system. Consequently, some of the more technical points have been omitted from this discussion. When actually classifying a wetland, the reader is advised to refer to the official classification document (Cowardin, *et al.* 1979) and should not rely solely on this overview.

The Service's wetland classification system is hierarchial or vertical in nature proceeding from general to specific, as noted in Figure 3. In this approach, wetlands are first defined at a rather broad level - the SYSTEM. The term SYSTEM represents "a complex of wetlands and deepwater habitats that share the influence of similar hydrologic, geomorphologic, chemical, or biological factors." Five systems are defined: Marine, Estuarine, Riverine, Lacustrine and Palustrine. The Marine System generally consists of the open ocean and its associated coastline, while the Estuarine System encompasses salt and brackish marshes and brackish waters of coastal rivers and embayments. Freshwater wetlands and deepwater habitats fall into one of the other three systems: Riverine (e.g., rivers and streams), Lacustrine, (e.g., lakes, reservoirs and large ponds) or Palustrine (e.g., marshes, bogs, swamps and small shallow ponds). Thus, at the most general level, wetlands can be defined as either Marine, Estuarine, Riverine, Lacustrine or Palustrine (Figure 4).

Each system, with the exception of the Palustrine, is further subdivided into subsystems. The Marine and Estuarine Systems both have the same two subsystems, which are defined by tidal water levels: (1) Subtidal - continuously submerged areas and (2) Intertidal - areas alternately flooded by tides and exposed to air. Sim-ilarly, the Lacustrine System is separated into two systems based on water depth: (1) Littoral - wetlands extending from the lake shore to a depth of 6.6 feet (2m) below low water or to the extent of nonpersistent emergents (e.g., arrowheads, pickerelweed or spatter-dock) if they grow beyond that depth, and (2) Limnetic - deepwater habitats lying beyond 6.6 feet (2m) at low water. By contrast, the Riverine System is further defined by four subsystems that represent different reaches of a flowing freshwater or lotic system: (1) Tidal - water levels subject to tidal fluctuations, (2) Lower Perennial - permanent, slow-flowing waters with a well-developed floodplain, (3) Upper Perennial - permanent, fast-flowing water with very little or no floodplain development, and (4) Intermittent - channel containing nontidal flowing water for only part of the year.

Below the subsystem, we encounter the CLASS level which describes the general appearance of the wetland or deepwater habitat in terms of the dominant vegetative life form or the composition of the substrate, where vegetative cover is less than 30% (Table 2). Of the 11 classes, five refer to areas where vegetation covers 30% or more of the surface: Aquatic Bed, Moss-Lichen Wetland, Emergent Wetland, Scrub-Shrub Wetland and Forested Wetland. The remaining six classes represent areas generally lacking vegetation, where the composition of the substrate and degree of flooding distinguish classes: Rock Bottom, Unconsolidated Bottom, Reef (sedentary invertebrate colony), Streambed, Rocky Shore, and Unconsolidated Shore. Permanently flooded unvegetated areas are classified as either Rock Bottom or Unconsolidated Bottom, while exposed areas are typed as Streambed, Rocky Shore or Unconsolidated Shore. Invertebrate reefs are found in both permanently flooded and exposed areas.

Each class is further divided into subclasses to better define the type of substrate in unvegetated areas (e.g., bedrock, rubble, cobble-gravel, mud, sand, and organic) or the type of dominant vegetation (e.g., persistent or nonpersistent emergents, moss, lichen, or broad-leaved deciduous, needle-leaved deciduous, broad-leaved evergreen, needle-leaved evergreen and dead woody plants). Below the subclass level, dominance type can be applied to specify the predominant plant or animal in the wetland community.

To allow better description of a given wetland or deepwater habitat in regard to hydrologic, chemical and soil characteristics and to human impacts, the classification system contains four types of specific modifiers: (1) Water Regime, (2) Water Chemistry, (3) Soil, and (4) Special. These modifiers may be applied to class and lower levels of the classification hierarchy.

8

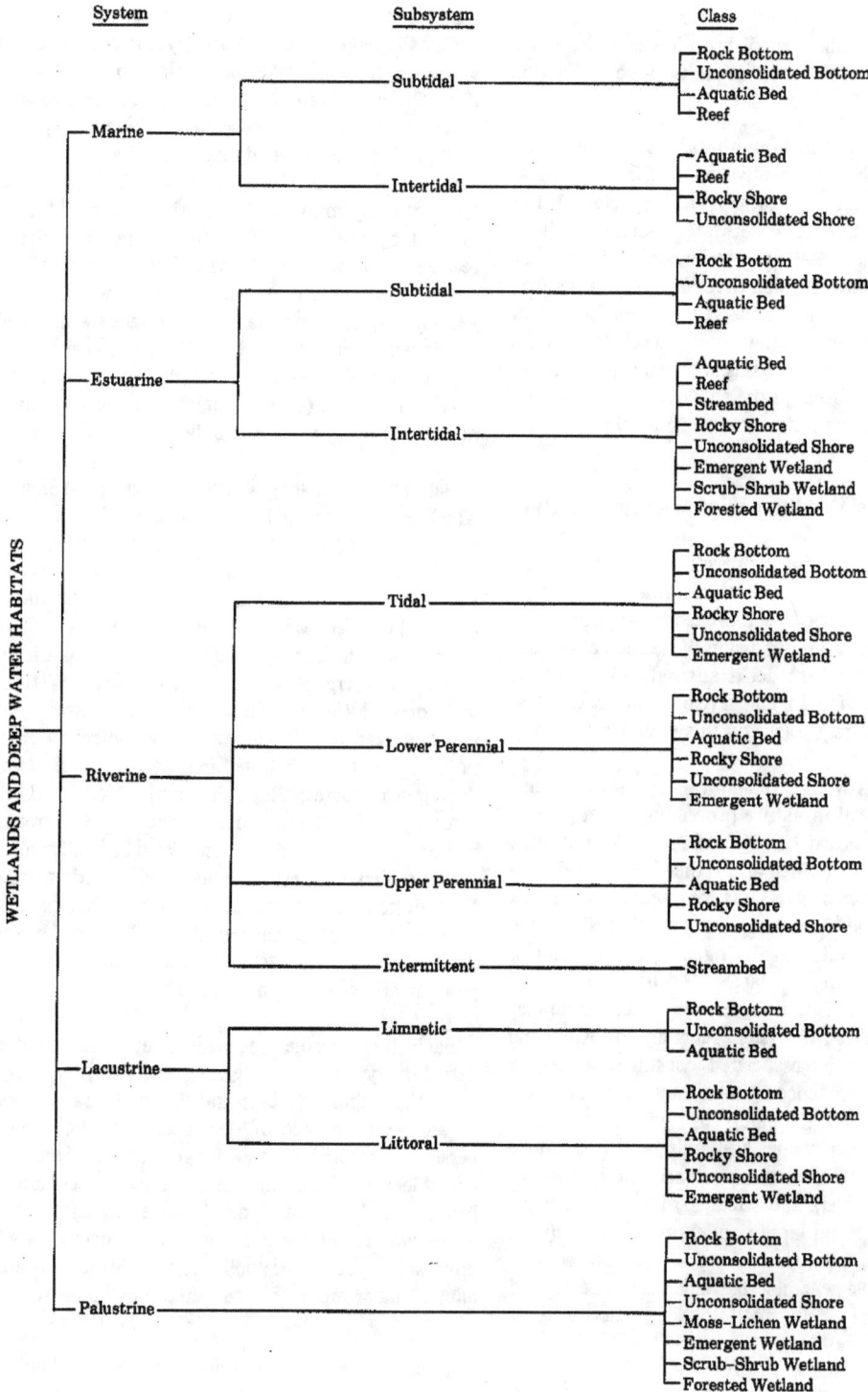

Figure 3. Classification hierarchy of wetlands and deepwater habitats showing systems, subsystems, and classes. The Palustrine System does not include deepwater habitats (Cowardin, *et al.* 1979).

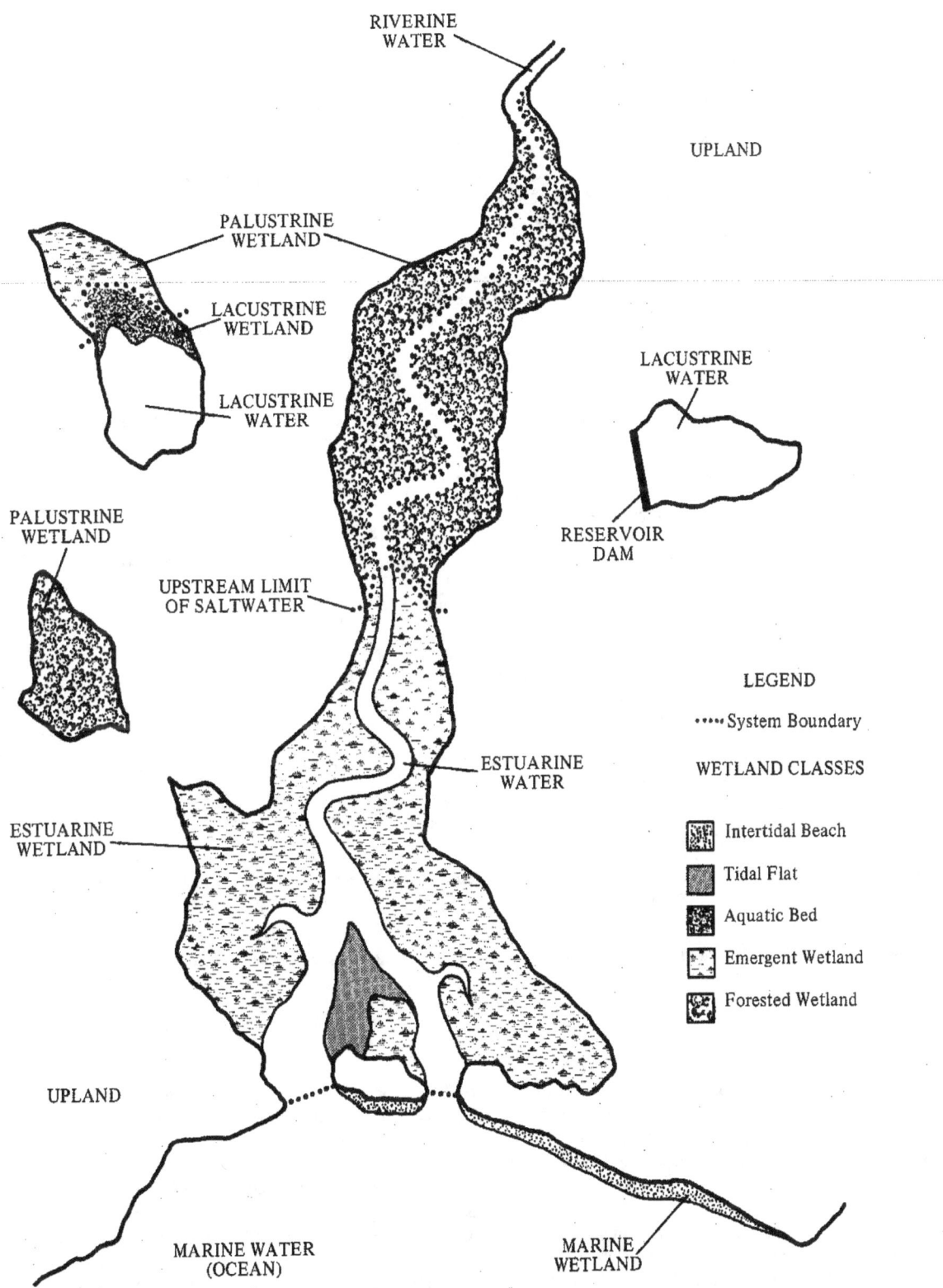

RIVERINE
WATER

UPLAND

PALUSTRINE
WETLAND

LACUSTRINE
WETLAND

LACUSTRINE
WATER

LACUSTRINE
WATER

PALUSTRINE
WETLAND

UPSTREAM LIMIT
OF SALTWATER

RESERVOIR
DAM

LEGEND

••••• System Boundary

WETLAND CLASSES

ESTUARINE
WATER

ESTUARINE
WETLAND

Intertidal Beach

Tidal Flat

Aquatic Bed

Emergent Wetland

Forested Wetland

UPLAND

MARINE WATER
(OCEAN)

MARINE
WETLAND

Figure 4. Diagram showing major wetland and deepwater habitat systems. Predominant wetland classes for each system are also designated.

Table 2. Classes and subclasses of wetlands and deepwater habitats (Cowardin, *et al.* 1979).

Class	Brief Description	Subclasses
Rock Bottom	Generally permanently flooded areas with bottom substrates consisting of at least 75% stones and boulders and less than 30% vegetative cover.	Bedrock; Rubble
Unconsolidated Bottom	Generally permanently flooded areas with bottom substrates consisting of at least 25% particles smaller than stones and less than 30% vegetative cover.	Cobble-Gravel; Sand; Mud; Organic
Aquatic Bed	Generally permanently flooded areas vegetated by plants growing principally on or below the water surface line.	Algal; Aquatic Moss; Rooted Vascular; Floating Vascular
Reef	Ridge-like or mound-like structures formed by the colonization and growth of sedentary invertebrates.	Coral; Mollusk; Worm
Streambed	Channel whose bottom is completed dewatered at low water periods.	Bedrock; Rubble; Cobble-Gravel; Sand; Mud; Organic; Vegetated
Rocky Shore	Wetlands characterized by bedrock, stones or boulders with areal coverage of 75% or more and with less than 30% coverage by vegetation.	Bedrock; Rubble
Unconsolidated Shore*	Wetlands having unconsolidated substrates with less than 75% coverage by stone, boulders and bedrock and less than 30% vegetative cover, except by pioneer plants. (*NOTE: This class combines two classes of the 1977 operational draft system - Beach/Bar and Flat. Beach/Bar is a sloping landform, while Flat is a nearly level landform.)	Cobble-Gravel; Sand; Mud; Organic; Vegetated
Moss-Lichen Wetland	Wetlands dominated by mosses or lichens where other plants have less than 30% coverage.	Moss; Lichen
Emergent Wetland	Wetlands dominated by erect, rooted, herbaceous hydrophytes.	Persistent; Nonpersistent
Scrub-Shrub Wetland	Wetlands dominated by woody vegetation less than 20 feet (6 m) tall.	Broad-leaved Deciduous; Needle-leaved Deciduous; Broad-leaved Evergreen; Needle-leaved Evergreen; Dead
Forested Wetland	Wetlands dominated by woody vegetation greater than 20 feet (6 m) tall.	Broad-leaved Deciduous; Needle-leaved Deciduous; Broad-leaved Evergreen; Needle-leaved Evergreen; Dead

Water regime modifiers describe flooding or soil saturation conditions and are divided into two main groups: (1) tidal and (2) nontidal. Tidal water regimes are used where water level fluctuations are largely driven by oceanic tides. Tidal regimes can be subdivided into two general categories, one for salt and brackish water tidal areas and another for freshwater tidal areas. This distinction is needed because of the special importance of seasonal river overflow in freshwater tidal areas. By contrast, nontidal modifiers define conditions where surface water runoff, ground-water discharge, and/or wind effects (i.e., lake seiches) cause water level changes. Both tidal and nontidal water regime modifiers are presented and briefly defined in Table 3.

Water chemistry modifiers are divided into two categories which describe the water's salinity or hydrogen ion concentration (pH): (1) salinity modifiers and (2) pH modifiers. Like water regimes, salinity modifiers have been further subdivided into two groups: halinity modifiers for tidal areas and salinity modifiers for nontidal areas. Estuarine and marine waters are

Table 3. Water regime modifiers, both tidal and nontidal groups (Cowardin, *et al.* 1979). An asterisk (*) denotes a water regime developed by the National Wetlands Inventory Group for mapping purposes.

Group	Type of Water	Water Regime	Definition
Tidal	Saltwater and brackish areas	Subtidal	Permanently flooded by tides.
		Irregularly exposed	Exposed less often than daily by tides.
		Regularly flooded	Daily tidal flooding and exposure to air.
		Irregularly flooded	Flooded less often than daily and typically exposed to air.
	Freshwater areas	Permanently flooded-tidal	Permanently flooded by tides or exposed less often than daily by tides.
		Regularly flooded-tidal	Daily tidal flooding and exposure to air.
		Seasonally flooded-tidal	Flooded irregularly by tides and seasonally by river overflow.
		Temporarily flooded-tidal	Flooded irregularly by tides and for brief periods during growing season by river overflow.
Nontidal	Inland freshwater and saline areas	Permanently flooded	Flooded through the year in all years.
		Intermittently exposed	Flooded year-round except during extreme droughts.
		Semipermanently flooded	Flooded throughout the growing season in most years.
		Seasonally flooded	Flooded for extended periods in growing season, but surface water is usually absent by end of growing season.
		Saturated	Surface water is seldom present, but substrate is saturated to the surface for most of the season.
		*Seasonally flooded/ saturated	Flooded for extended periods during growing season and when surface water is absent, water table remains at or very near the soil surface.
		Temporarily flooded	Flooded for only brief periods during growing season, with water table usually well below the soil surface for most of the season.
		Intermittently flooded	Substrate is usually exposed and only flooded for variable periods without detectable seasonal periodicity (not always wetland; may be upland in some situations).
		Artificially flooded	Duration and amount of flooding is controlled by means of pumps or siphons in combination with dikes or dams.

Table 4. Salinity modifiers for coastal and inland areas (Cowardin, *et al.* 1979).

Coastal Modifiers[1]	Inland Modifiers[2]	Salinity (o/oo)	Approximate Specific Conductance (Mhos at 25 °C)
Hyperhaline	Hypersaline	>40	>60,000
Euhaline	Eusaline	30-40	45,000-60,000
Mixohaline (Brackish)	Mixosaline[3]	0.5-30	800-45,000
Polyhaline	Polysaline	18-30	30,000-45,000
Mesohaline	Mesosaline	5-18	8,000-30,000
Oligohaline	Oligosaline	0.5-5	800-8,000
Fresh	Fresh	<0.5	<800

[1] Coastal modifiers are employed in the Marine and Estuarine Systems.

[2] Inland modifiers are employed in the Riverine, Lacustrine and Palustrine Systems.

[3] The term "brackish" should not be used for inland wetlands or deepwater habitats.

dominated by sodium chloride, which is gradually diluted by fresh water as one moves upstream in coastal rivers. On the other hand, the salinity of inland waters is dominated by four major cations (i.e., calcium, magnesium, sodium and potassium) and three major anions (i.e., carbonate, sulfate, and chloride). Interactions between precipitation, surface runoff, groundwater flow, evaporation, and sometimes plant evapotranspiration form inland salts. Table 4 shows ranges of halinity and salinity modifiers which are a modification of the Venice System (Remane and Schlieper 1971). The other set of water chemistry modifiers are pH modifiers for identifying acid (pH<5.5), circumneutral (5.5-7.4) and alkaline (pH>7.4) waters. Some studies have shown a good correlation between plant distribution and pH levels (Sjors 1950; Jeglum 1971). Moreover, pH can be used to distinguish between mineral-rich and mineral-poor wetlands.

The third group of modifiers - soil modifiers - are presented because the nature of the soil exerts strong influences on plant growth and reproduction as well as on the animals living in it. Two soil modifiers are given: (1) mineral and (2) organic. In general, if a soil has 20% or more organic matter by weight in the upper 16 inches, it is considered an organic soil, whereas if it has less than this amount, it is a mineral soil. For specific definitions, please refer to Appendix D of the Service's classification system (Cowardin, *et al.* 1979) or to **Soil Taxonomy** (U.S.D.A. Soil Conservation Service 1975).

The final set of modifiers - special modifiers - were established to describe the activities of people or beaver affecting wetlands and deepwater habitats. These modifiers include: excavated, impounded (i.e., to obstruct outflow of water), diked (i.e., to obstruct inflow of water), partly drained, farmed, and artificial (i.e., materials deposited to create or modify a wetland or deepwater habitat).

References

Cowardin, L.M., V. Carter, F.C. Golet and E.T. LaRoe. 1977. Classification of Wetlands and Deep-water Habitats of the United States (An Operational Draft). U.S. Fish and Wildlife Service. October 1977. 100 pp.

Cowardin, L.M., V. Carter, F.C. Golet and E.T. LaRoe. 1979. Classification of Wetlands and Deepwater Habitats of the United States. U.S. Fish and Wildlife Service. FWS/OBS-79/31. 103 pp.

Gopal, B., R.E. Turner, R.G. Wetzel and D.F. Whigham. 1982. Wetlands Ecology and Management. Proceedings of the First International Wetlands Conference (September 10-17, 1980; New Delhi, India). National Institute of Ecology and International Scientific Publications, Jaipur, India. 514 pp.

Jeglum, J.K. 1971. Plant indicators of pH and water level in peat lands at Candle Lake, Saskatchewan. Can. J. Bot. 49: 1661-1676.

Martin, A.C., N. Hotchkiss, F.M. Uhler and W.S. Bourn. 1953. Classification of Wetlands of the United States. U.S. Fish and Wildlife Service. Special Scientific Report, Wildlife No. 20. 14 pp.

Remane, A. and C. Schlieper. 1971. Biology of Brackish Water. Wiley Interscience Division, John Wiley & Sons, New York. 372 pp.

Sather, J.H. (editor). 1976. Proceedings of the National Wetland Classification and Inventory Workshop, July 20-23, 1975, at the University of Maryland. U.S. Fish and Wildlife Service. 358 pp.

Shaw, S.P. and C.G. Fredine. 1956. Wetlands of the United States. U.S. Fish and Wildlife Service. Circular 39. 67 pp.

Sjors, H. 1950. On the relation between vegetation and electrolytes in north Swedish mire waters. Oikos 2: 241-258.

U.S. Fish and Wildlife Service. 1976. Existing State and Local Wetlands Surveys (1965-1975). Volume II. Narrative. Office of Biological Services, Washington, DC. 453 pp.

U.S.D.A. Soil Conservation Service. 1975. Soil Taxonomy. Department of Agriculture. Agriculture Handbook No. 436. 754 pp.

CHAPTER 3.

National Wetlands Inventory
Mapping Techniques and Results

Introduction

The National Wetlands Inventory Project (NWI) relies heavily on remote sensing techniques and field investigations for wetlands identification and mapping. High-altitude aerial photography ranging in scale from 1:60,000 to 1:80,000 serves as the primary remote imagery source. Once suitable high-altitude photography is obtained, there are seven major steps in preparing wetland maps: (1) field investigations, (2) photo interpretation, (3) review of existing wetland information, (4) quality assurance, (5) draft map production, (6) interagency review of draft maps, and (7) final map production. Steps 1, 2 and 3 encompass the basic data collection phase of the inventory. Upon publication of final wetland maps for Delaware, the Service constructed a wetland database, where all NWI maps were digitized and data entered into a computer. This database generated acreage summaries on wetlands and deepwater habitats on a county basis. The procedures used to inventory Delaware's wetlands and the results of this inventory are discussed in the following sections.

Wetlands Inventory Techniques
Review of Existing Wetlands Inventories

Prior to initiating the National Wetlands Inventory in Delaware in 1982, the Service reviewed past wetlands surveys to ensure that no duplication would occur. Major inventories included the Service's survey of important waterfowl wetlands in 1953 and coastal wetlands in 1959 and 1965, and coastal wetland mapping by the University of Delaware in 1973 and 1976 (Klemas, *et al.* 1973; Daiber, *et al.* 1976). Although the state's coastal wetlands were mapped in great detail, no comparable mapping existed for inland wetlands. The NWI would fulfill this data gap by conducting a comprehensive inventory of Delaware's wetland resources. An updated summary of major wetlands inventories in Delaware is presented in Table 5.

Mapping Photography

For mapping Delaware's wetlands, the Service used 1:60,000 color infrared photography for nearly all of the state (Figure 5). Most of this imagery was acquired from the spring of 1981 to the spring of 1982. Thus, the effective date of this inventory can be considered 1981-82.

Photo Interpretation and Collateral Data

Photo interpretation was performed by the Department of Forestry and Wildlife Management, University of Massachusetts, Amherst. All photo interpretation was done in stereo using mirror and binocular stereoscopes. Other collateral data sources used to aid in wetland detection and classification included:

(1) U.S. Geological Survey topographic maps;
(2) U.S.D.A. Soil Conservation Service soil surveys;
(3) U.S. Department of Commerce coastal and geodetic survey maps;
(4) **An Atlas of Delaware's Wetlands and Estuarine Resources** (Daiber, *et al.* 1976);
(5) **Coastal Vegetation of Delaware** (Klemas, *et al.* 1973);
(6) **Extent of Brackish Water in the Tidal Rivers of Maryland** (Webb and Heidel 1970).

Wetland photo interpretation, although extremely efficient and accurate for inventorying wetlands, does have certain limitations. Consequently, some problems arose during the course of the survey. Additional field work or use of collateral data was necessary to overcome these constraints. These problems and their resolution are discussed below.

1. Delineation of high marsh vs. low marsh in estuarine areas. Several areas appeared to be low marsh on the aerial photography. Field checks were conducted where access was available. Wetland experts with the Delaware Department of Natural Resources and Environmental Control and the University of Delaware were consulted as well as available research reports (Klemas, *et al.* 1973; Daiber, *et al.* 1976). The consensus was that low marsh communities dominated by the tall form of smooth cordgrass (*Spartina alterniflora*) are not abundant in Delaware and are primarily restricted to creekbanks, although extensive areas are locally present within Woodland Wildlife Management Area and Bombay Hook National Wildlife Refuge.

Table 5. Wetlands inventories conducted in Delaware. This list represents the more significant surveys and does not include local studies.

Date of Survey	Lead Agency	Wetlands Mapped	Comments
1982-84	U.S. Fish & Wildlife Service	Coastal and inland wetlands	First comprehensive inventory of Delaware's wetland and deepwater habitat resources. Wetland maps produced at 1:24,000. Wetlands classified according to Cowardin, *et al.* (1977). Minimum mapping unit = 1 acre. Identified approximately 223,000 acres of wetlands. Final report (Tiner 1985).
1981	University of Delaware and Delaware Dept. of Natural Resources and Environmental Control	Coastal wetlands	Produced updated regulatory maps. Identified current human-induced loss rate of 20 ac/yr and natural gains (7 ac/yr) and losses (10 ac/yr) from 1973 to 1979. Journal article published (Hardisky and Klemas 1983).
1976	University of Delaware and Delaware State Planning Office	Coastal wetlands	An atlas of coastal wetland maps (Daiber, *et al.* 1976). Identified 83,420 acres in 1973 and 91,672 acres in 1938, for a net loss of 9%.
1973	University of Delaware and Delaware Dept. of Natural Resources and Environmental Control	Coastal wetlands	Regulatory maps produced. Report (Klemas, *et al.* 1973).
1965	U.S. Fish & Wildlife Service	Coastal wetlands	Resurvey of coastal marshes. Identified 115,501 acres in 1964 and loss of 1,412 acres (1959-64). Report (FWS 1965).
1959	U.S. Fish & Wildlife Service	Coastal wetlands	Resurvey of high and moderate value wetlands and all tidal wetlands. Identified 120,061 acres in 1959 and loss of 3,148 acres (1954-59). Report (FWS 1959).
1953	U.S. Fish & Wildlife Service	Coastal and inland wetlands of importance to waterfowl	Not comprehensive; focused on 90% of the wetlands important to waterfowl. Minimum mapping unit = 40 acres. Identified 131,275 acres in 1953. Report (FWS 1953).

2. Brackish/freshwater and tidal/nontidal boundary breaks and associated wetland classification. Field checks were conducted and a report on the extent of brackish waters in Maryland (Webb and Heidel 1970) which shows the Chesapeake Bay side of Delaware was consulted to make these breaks. Boundaries should be considered approximate. Many impoundments were observed in the upper reaches of tidal waters particularly in rivers draining into Delaware Bay. This situation presented a clearly defined boundary between tidal and nontidal waters.

3. Water regime determination and wetland/upland breaks in forested areas. Channelization projects and drainage ditches have impacted many forested wetlands. Differentiating between totally drained and partially drained forested wetlands initially posed a problem, but subtle photo signatures were identified through field checking and reference to soil surveys that favorably resolved this problem.

4. Delineation of intertidal flats. The photography used for the inventory was not tide-coordinated, so all intertidal flats were not visible. Collateral tide-coordinated photography was available for a few quadrangles in the Mispillion River area. The remainder of the tidal flats were identified from coastal and geodetic survey maps and topographic maps.

5. Problem associated with tidal flooding. Photography used for this survey was not tide-coordinated, therefore, on rare occasions, some emergent wetlands may have been obscured by flooding waters. In these situations, undetected emergent wetlands may be included as part of the open water class in estuarine and riverine (tidal) systems.

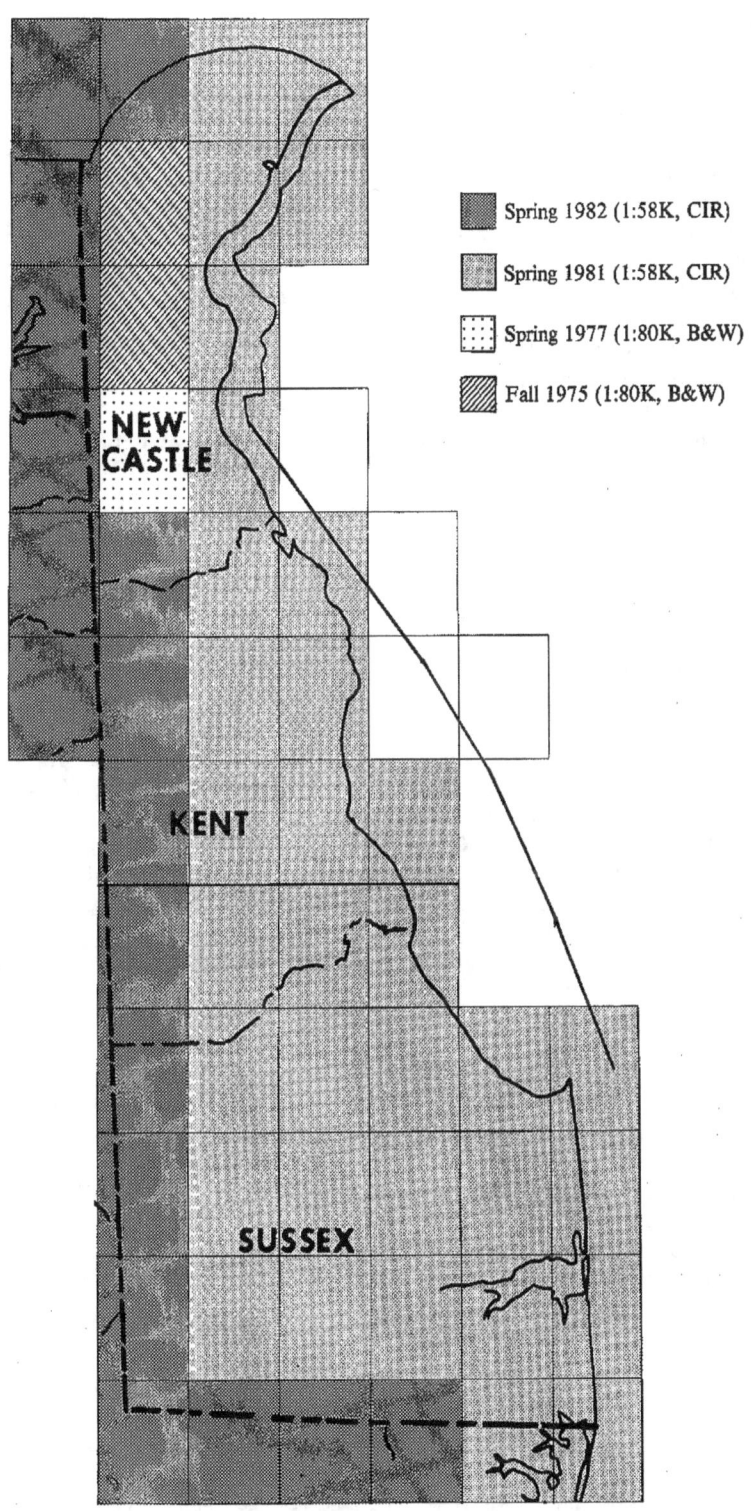

Spring 1982 (1:58K, CIR)

Spring 1981 (1:58K, CIR)

Spring 1977 (1:80K, B&W)

Fall 1975 (1:80K, B&W)

NEW CASTLE

KENT

SUSSEX

Figure 5. Index of aerial photography used for the National Wetlands Inventory in Delaware.

6. Identification of freshwater aquatic beds and nonpersistent emergent wetlands. Due to use of spring photography in many areas, aquatic beds in freshwater ponds and lakes and nonpersistent emergent wetlands in riverine tidal areas were not identifiable. These wetlands were, therefore, classified as open water or as riverine tidal flats, respectively. Maps, however, do show some aquatic beds and nonpersistent emergent wetlands where observed during field investigations.

7. Inclusion of small upland areas within wetland boundaries. Small islands of higher elevations and better drained upland areas naturally exist within many wetlands. Due to minimum mapping units, small upland areas may be included within designated wetlands. Field inspections and/or use of larger-scale photography can be used to refine wetland boundaries when necessary.

8. Problem associated with "pothole" flooding. Isolated depressional wetlands called "potholes" are prevalent in central-western Delaware near Kenton. Many of these wetlands were flooded at the time that the aerial photographs were taken. As a result, persistent vegetation within these basins was not apparent. To identify the vegetation, subtle photo signatures were found that appeared to correlate well with various wetland symbols on the U.S.G.S. topographic maps. Subsequent field checking confirmed reliable results following this procedure.

Field Investigations

Ground truthing surveys were conducted to collect information on plant communities of various wetlands and to gain confidence in detecting and classifying wetlands from aerial photography. Detailed notes were taken at more than 100 sites throughout the state. In addition to these sites, observations were made at countless other wetlands for classification purposes and notations were recorded on appropriate topographic maps. In total, approximately five weeks were spent in the field studying wetlands.

Draft Map Production

Upon completion of photo interpretation, two levels of quality assurance were performed: (1) regional quality control, and (2) national consistency quality assurance. Regional review of each interpreted photo was accomplished by Regional Office's NWI staff to ensure identification of all wetlands and proper classification. By contrast, national quality control by the NWI Group at St. Petersburg, Florida entailed spot checking of photos to ensure that national standards have been successfully followed. Once approved by quality assurance, draft large-scale (1:24,000) wetland maps were produced by the Group's support service contractor using Bausch and Lomb zoom transfer scopes.

Draft Map Review

Draft maps were sent to the following agencies for review and comment:

(1) U.S. Fish and Wildlife Service, Annapolis Field Office;
(2) U.S. Army Corps of Engineers (Philadelphia District);
(3) U.S.D.A. Soil Conservation Service;
(4) U.S. Environmental Protection Agency (Region III);
(5) National Marine Fisheries Service;
(6) Delaware Dept. of Natural Resources and Environmental Control, Wetlands Section.

In addition, the Regional Office's NWI staff conducted field checks and a thorough examination of draft maps to ensure proper placement of wetland polygons and labels as well as accurate classification.

Final Map Production

All comments received were evaluated and incorporated into the final maps, as appropriate. Final maps were published in 1982-83.

Wetland Database Construction

Upon publication of the final wetland maps in early 1983, the Service started construction of a statewide wetland database by digitizing these maps. The database and its applications are described by Tiner and Pywell (1983). The database was created by January 1984 which allowed generation of county and statewide wetland acreage summaries and gave the Service the capability to produce color-coded wetland maps for specific areas. Duplicate tapes of this wetland database will be given to the Delaware Department of Natural Resources and Environmental Control.

Financial Contributors

The Delaware Department of Natural Resources and Environmental Control (Wetlands Section) and the Philadelphia District of the U.S. Army Corps of Engineers provided financial support to produce the NWI maps for Delaware. The state also contributed nearly all of the funds for creating the statewide wetland database.

Wetlands Inventory Results

National Wetlands Inventory Maps

A total of 54-1:24,000 wetland maps were produced. These maps identify the size, shape and type of wetlands and deepwater habitats in accordance with NWI specifications. The minimum mapping unit for wetlands is approximately 1 acre. A recent evaluation of NWI maps in Massachusetts determined that these maps had accuracies exceeding 95% (Swartwout, *et al.* 1982). This high accuracy is possible because the inventory technique involves a combination of photo interpretation, field studies, use of existing information and interagency review of draft maps. Final maps have been available since the summer of 1983. Figure 6 shows an example of the large-scale map. In the near future, a series of small-scale wetland maps (1:100,000) will be produced by the NWI. Copies of NWI maps and a map catalogue can be ordered from the Delaware Department of Natural Resources and Environmental Control, Wetlands Section, 89 Kings Highway, P.O. Box 1401, Dover, DE 19903 (302-736-4691).

Wetland and Deepwater Habitat Acreage Summaries

State Totals

According to our survey, Delaware possesses roughly 223,000 acres of wetlands and 234,000 acres of deepwater habitats, excluding marine waters and smaller rivers and streams that either appear as linear features on wetlands maps or wetlands that were not identified due to their small size. About 18% of the state's land surface is represented by wetlands.

The relative extent of major wetland types is shown in Figure 7. About 96% of the state's wetlands fall within two systems - palustrine (56%) and estuarine (40%). The general distribution of Delaware's wetlands and deepwater habitats is shown on the enclosed figure at the back of this report.

Of the 89,758 estuarine wetland acres, 86% are emergent wetlands. Most of these are salt and brackish marshes (73,589 acres), while 4,494 acres of slightly brackish or oligohaline marshes were inventoried. Ninety percent of the estuarine emergent wetlands are irregularly flooded, with the remainder subject to daily tidal flooding. Nearly 38% of these wetlands have been mosquito ditched. Intertidal flats accounted for 8,872 acres and scrub-shrub wetlands for only 929 acres. A total of 1,874 acres of estuarine beaches were found.

Palustrine wetlands, covering 131,902 acres, are about 1.5 times more abundant than estuarine wetlands. Most of this acreage (95% or 124,781 acres) is represented by nontidal freshwater wetlands, with the remainder being tidally-influenced. Almost 90% of the nontidal wetlands are forested wetlands, which are mostly red maple swamps. Interestingly, nontidal evergreen forested wetlands total only 13,068 acres, with over 90% occurring in Sussex County and largely dominated by loblolly pine. Also, 12% of the state's nontidal forested wetlands have been channelized or ditched. Emergent wetlands (5,994 acres), scrub-shrub wetlands (4,019 acres) and shallow ponds (3,118 acres) comprise nearly all of the remaining palustrine nontidal wetlands. From a water regime standpoint, about 60% of the state's nontidal wetlands are temporarily flooded and 37% are seasonally flooded.

Freshwater tidal wetlands are rather limited, representing only 3.5% of the state's wetland resource. Only 7,774 acres of freshwater tidal flats, and emergent, shrub and forested wetlands were inventoried. Most of these wetlands are seasonally flooded-tidal palustrine wetlands, with forested wetlands alone representing about 55% of all freshwater tidal wetlands. Only 653 acres of riverine tidal wetlands were mapped.

Deepwater habitat acreage in Delaware totals 234,215 acres, excluding marine waters. Most of this (98% or 228,660 acres) is represented by estuarine or brackish tidal waters of bays and coastal rivers. Freshwater tidal waters amount to 856 acres, while other rivers total only 200 acres. Lakes and reservoirs cover 4,499 acres.

County Totals

Acreages of wetlands and deepwater habitats for each county are shown in Tables 6 and 7, respectively. More detailed county acreage summaries for wetland types classified to water regime are presented in Table 8. Sussex County has the largest extent of wetlands (98,141 acres) and is closely followed by Kent County (87,894 acres), with New Castle County far behind with only

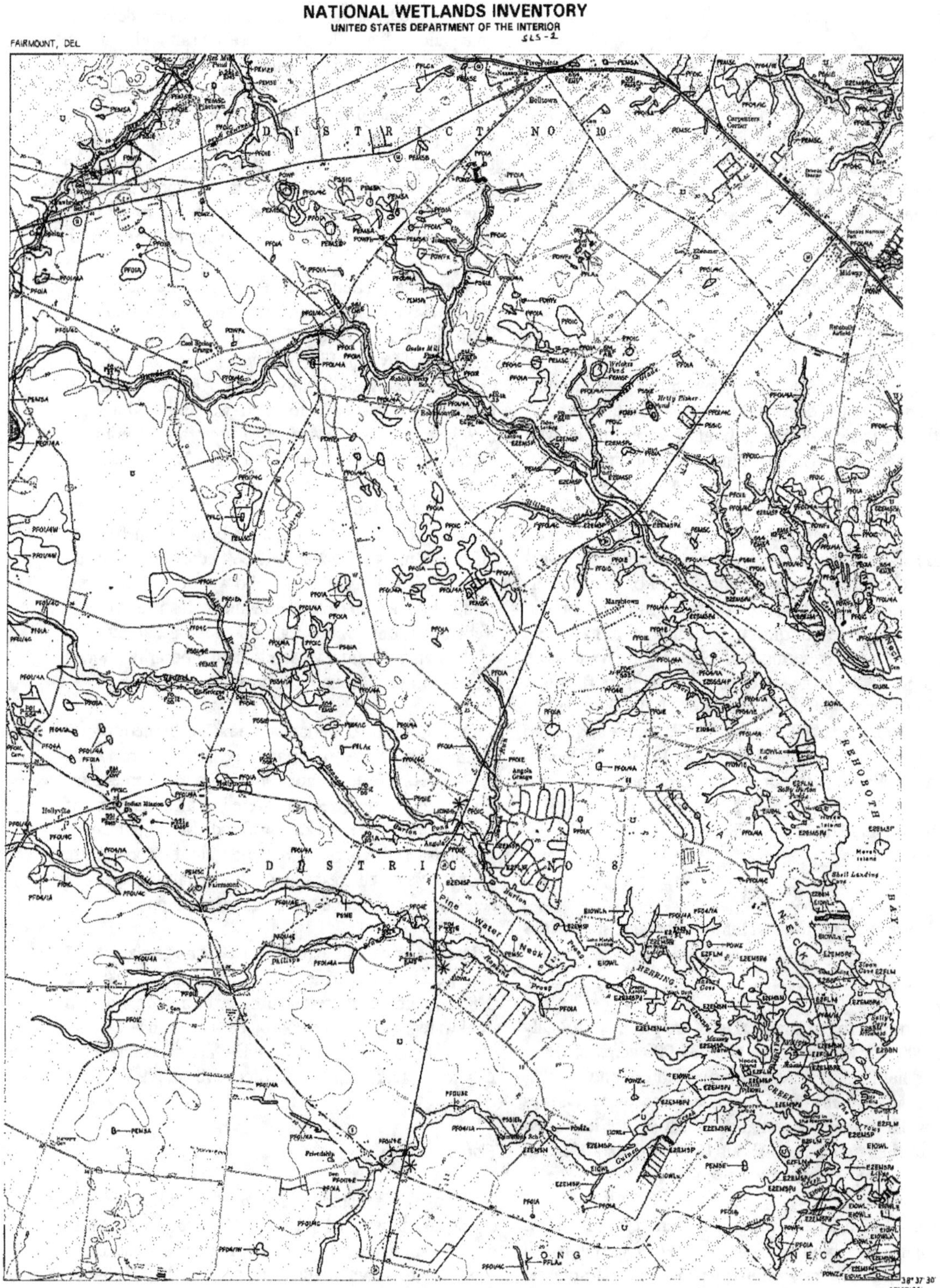

18

Figure 6. Example of a National Wetlands Inventory map. This is a reduction of a 1:24,000 scale map, with the legend omitted.

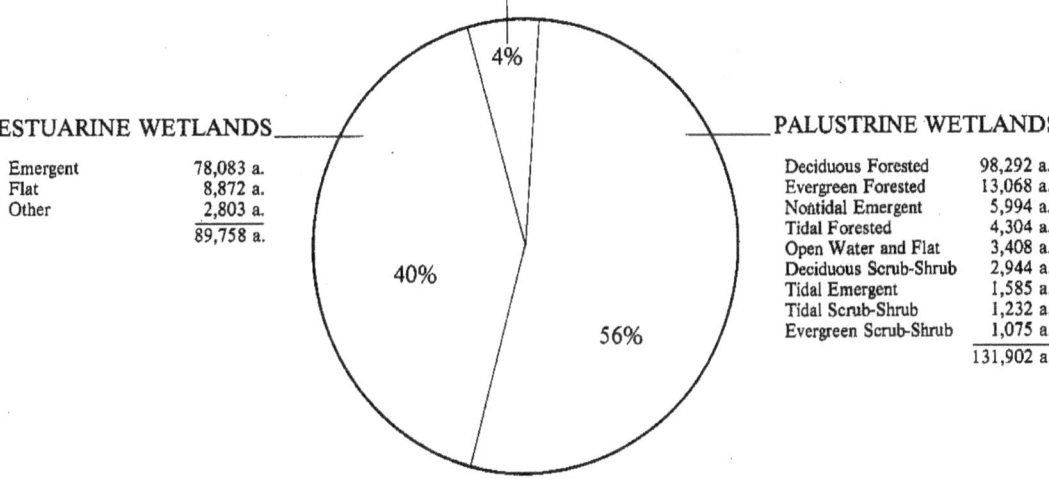

MARINE, RIVERINE, and LACUSTRINE WETLANDS (1,333 a.)

4%

ESTUARINE WETLANDS

Emergent	78,083 a.
Flat	8,872 a.
Other	2,803 a.
	89,758 a.

40%

56%

PALUSTRINE WETLANDS

Deciduous Forested	98,292 a.
Evergreen Forested	13,068 a.
Nontidal Emergent	5,994 a.
Tidal Forested	4,304 a.
Open Water and Flat	3,408 a.
Deciduous Scrub-Shrub	2,944 a.
Tidal Emergent	1,585 a.
Tidal Scrub-Shrub	1,232 a.
Evergreen Scrub-Shrub	1,075 a.
	131,902 a.

Figure 7. Relative extent of Delaware's wetlands.

Table 6. Wetland acreage summaries for Delaware counties.

SYSTEM	KENT COUNTY (land area = 380,160 acres)	NEW CASTLE COUNTY (land area = 280,320 acres)	SUSSEX COUNTY (land area = 608,000 acres)
Marine Beaches/Bars	—	—	540 acres
Estuarine Wetlands			
Beaches/Bars	374 acres	135 acres	1,365 acres
Intertidal Flats	586 acres	6,596 acres	1,690 acres
Emergent Wetlands	39,607 acres	17,005 acres	21,471 acres
Scrub-Shrub Wetlands	375 acres	22 acres	532 acres
Estuarine Total	40,942 acres	23,758 acres	25,058 acres
Riverine Tidal Wetlands	184 acres	5 acres	464 acres
Palustrine Wetlands			
Tidal Wetlands	1,493 acres	744 acres	4,884 acres
Open Water/Flats	769 acres	1,247 acres	1,392 acres
Emergent Wetlands	1,649 acres	2,508 acres	1,837 acres
Scrub-Shrub Wetlands	1,361 acres	537 acres	2,121 acres
Forested Wetlands	41,484 acres	8,059 acres	61,817 acres
Palustrine Total	46,756 acres	13,095 acres	72,051 acres
Lacustrine Wetlands	12 acres	100 acres	28 acres
Total	87,894 acres (23% of the County)	36,958 acres (13% of the County)	98,141 acres (16% of the County)

Table 7. Acreage summaries for deepwater habitats in Delaware by county.

County	Estuarine Waters	Riverine Waters	Lacustrine Waters		Deepwater Habitat Total
KENT	72,400 acres	183 acres	1,479 acres	=	74,062 acres
NEW CASTLE	34,812 acres	225 acres	1,310 acres	=	36,347 acres
SUSSEX	59,820 acres	648 acres	1,710 acres	=	62,178 acres
(Unmapped area of Delaware Bay)	61,628 acres	—	—	=	61,628 acres
STATE TOTAL	228,660 acres	1,056 acres	4,499 acres	=	234,215 acres

36,958 acres. If the percentage of the county occupied by wetlands is examined, Kent County leads the others with 23% the county being wetland.

The extent of ditching and channelization of wetlands in the counties showed an interesting trend. Sussex County had more extensive ditching in estuarine emergent wetlands than any other county with 75% of these marshes ditched for mosquito control. Kent County had 32% of these marshes ditched, while New Castle had only 2% ditched. Channelization and ditching of palustrine forested wetlands were most significant in Kent and Sussex Counties, with 14% and 13% of the forested wetlands affected. New Castle County had only 1% of these wetlands altered. It is interesting that the more rural counties had more ditching than urban New Castle County. Kent and Sussex Counties have more streams to provide outlets for drainage ditches and substantial acreages of bottom-land forested wetlands have been converted to cropland.

Kent County with much of the state's portion of Delaware Bay exceeds other counties in deepwater habitat acreage. Sussex County with the state's largest coastal embayments (i.e., Rehoboth Bay, Indian River Bay, and Little Assawoman Bay) is a close second. Lakes and deep ponds (lacustrine waters) are rather evenly distributed among the three counties. Sussex County has the largest extent of riverine waters.

Summary

The NWI Project has completed an inventory of Delaware's wetlands using aerial photo interpretation methods. Detailed wetland maps have been produced for the entire state. A wetland database has been constructed through computer mapping techniques. This database produced wetland acreage summaries for the state and for each county. Nearly 223,000 acres of wetland and 234,000 acres of deepwater habitat were inventoried in Delaware. Thus, about 18% of the state was represented by wetland.

Table 8. Acreage summaries of Delaware's wetlands by type, including water regime.

System	Wetland Type	Water Regime	Kent County (acres)	New Castle County (acres)	Sussex County (acres)	State Total (acres)
Marine	Beach/Bar	regularly/irregularly flooded	—	—	540	540
Estuarine	Beach/Bar	regularly/irregularly flooded	374	135	1,365	1,874
	Flat	regularly flooded	541	6,349	1,678	8,568
		regularly flooded (oligohaline)	45	247	12	304
	Emergent Wetland	regularly flooded	5,115	1,190	308	6,613
		regularly flooded (oligohaline)	120	1,043	137	1,300
		irregularly flooded	33,415	13,131	20,430	66,976
		irregularly flooded (oligohaline)	957	1,641	596	3,194
	Scrub-Shrub Wetland (Deciduous)	irregularly flooded	88	10	207	305
	Scrub-Shrub Wetland (Evergreen)	irregularly flooded	287	12	325	624
Riverine	Flat (Tidal)	regularly flooded	175	5	30	210
	Emergent Wetland (Tidal)	regularly flooded	9	—	434	443
Lacustrine	Open Water (Littoral)	permanently flooded	—	100	—	100
	Emergent Wetland	semipermanently flooded	12	—	28	40
Palustrine	Emergent Wetland (Tidal)	seasonally flooded-tidal	68	290	1,227	1,585
	Scrub-Shrub Wetland (Deciduous; Tidal)	seasonally flooded-tidal	87	136	421	644
	Scrub-Shrub Wetland (Evergreen; Tidal)	seasonally flooded-tidal	341	53	194	588
	Forested Wetland (Deciduous; Tidal)	seasonally flooded-tidal	987	257	2,846	4,090
	Forested Wetland (Evergreen; Tidal)	seasonally flooded-tidal	10	8	196	214
	Open Water (Nontidal)	permanently flooded	750	1,066	1,302	3,118
	Flat (Nontidal)	—	19	181	90	290
	Emergent Wetland	semipermanently flooded	409	487	251	1,147
		seasonally flooded	400	921	782	2,103
		temporarily flooded	840	1,100	804	2,744
	Scrub-Shrub Wetland (Deciduous)	semipermanently flooded	176	84	61	321
		seasonally flooded	302	293	615	1,210
		temporarily flooded	782	158	473	1,413
	Scrub-Shrub Wetland (Evergreen)	seasonally flooded	35	1	168	204
		temporarily flooded	66	1	804	871
	Forested Wetland (Deciduous)	seasonally flooded/saturated	4,069	879	11,415	16,363
		seasonally flooded	8,986	3,370	10,476	22,832
		temporarily flooded	27,352	3,759	27,691	58,802
	Forested Wetland (Bald Cypress)	seasonally flooded/saturated	—	—	295	295
	Forested Wetland (Evergreen)	seasonally flooded/saturated	44	4	1,251	1,299
		seasonally flooded	110	—	1,737	1,847
		temporarily flooded	923	47	8,952	9,922

References

Cowardin, L.M., V. Carter, F.C. Golet and E.T. LaRoe. 1977. Classification of Wetlands and Deep-water Habitats of the United States (An Operational Draft). U.S. Fish and Wildlife Service. October 1977. 100 pp.

Cowardin, L.M., V. Carter, F.C. Golet and E.T. LaRoe. 1979. Classification of Wetlands and Deepwater Habitats of the United States. U.S. Fish and Wildlife Service. FWS/OBS-79/31. 103 pp.

Daiber, F.C., L.L. Thornton, K.A. Bolster, T.G. Campbell, O.W. Crichton, G.L. Esposito, D.R. Jones, and J.M. Tyrawski. 1976. An Atlas of Delaware's Wetlands and Estuarine Resources. Del. Coastal Mgmt. Program. Tech. Rept. No. 2. 528 pp.

Hardisky, M.A. and V. Klemas. 1983. Tidal wetlands natural and human-made changes from 1973 to 1979 in Delaware: mapping techniques and results. Environ. Manag. 7(4): 1-6.

Klemas, V., F.C. Daiber, D.S. Bartlett, O.W. Crichton, and A.O. Fornes. 1973. Coastal Vegetation of Delaware. University of Delaware, Newark. 29 pp.

Swartwout, D.J., W.P. MacConnell, and J.T. Finn. 1982. An Evaluation of the National Wetlands Inventory in Massachusetts. Proc. of In-Place Resource Inventories Workshop (University of Maine, Orono, August 9-14, 1981). pp. 685-691.

Tiner, R.W., Jr. 1985. Wetlands of Delaware. U.S. Fish and Wildlife Service and Delaware Department of Natural Resources and Environmental Control. Cooperative Publication.

Tiner, R.W., Jr. and H.R. Pywell. 1983. Creating a national geo-referenced wetland data base for managing wetlands in the United States. Proc. of the National Conference on Resource Management Applications: Energy and Environment (August 23-27, San Francisco, CA). Vol. III: 103-115.

U.S. Fish and Wildlife Service. 1953. Wetlands Inventory of Delaware. Office of River Basin Studies, Region 5, Boston, MA.

U.S. Fish and Wildlife Service. 1959. A Supplementary Report on the Wetlands of Delaware. Office of River Basin Studies, Region 5, Boston, MA.

U.S. Fish and Wildlife Service. 1965. A Supplementary Report on the Coastal Wetlands Inventory of Delaware. Office of River Basin Studies, Region 5, Boston, MA. 13 pp.

U.S. Fish and Wildlife Service. 1981. Mapping Conventions for the National Wetlands Inventory. Mimeo. 30 pp.

Webb, W.E. and S.G. Heidel. 1970. Extent of Brackish Water in the Tidal Rivers of Maryland. Maryland Geol. Survey. Rept. of Invest. No. 12. 46 pp.

CHAPTER 4.

Wetland Hydrology

Introduction

The presence of water from flooding, surface water runoff, ground-water discharge, or ocean-driven tides is the driving force creating and maintaining wetlands. These hydrologic mechanisms determine the nature of the soils and the types of plants and animals living in wetlands. An accurate assessment of hydrology unfortunately requires extensive knowledge of the frequency and duration of flooding, water table fluctuations and ground-water relationships. This information can only be gained through intensive and long term studies. There are, however, ways to generally recognize differences in hydrology or water regime. At certain times of the year, such as during spring floods or high tides in coastal areas, hydrology is apparent. Yet, for most of the year, such obvious evidence is lacking in many wetlands. At these times, less conspicuous signs of flooding may be observed: (1) water marks on vegetation, (2) water-transported debris on plants or collected around their bases, and (3) water-stained leaves on the ground. These signs and knowledge of the water table and wetland vegetation help us recognize hydrologic differences between wetlands.

The Service's wetland classification system (Cowardin, *et al.* 1979) includes water regime modifiers to describe hydrologic characteristics. Two groups of water regimes are identified: (1) tidal and (2) nontidal. Tidal water regimes are driven by oceanic tides, while nontidal regimes are largely influenced by surface water runoff and ground-water discharge. The state of our knowledge in wetland hydrology has been reported by Carter and others (1979) and Leitch (1981). The hydrology and geology of Delaware's coastal zone have been described (Sundstrom, *et al.* 1975).

Tidal Wetland Hydrology

In coastal areas, ocean-driven tides are the dominant hydrologic feature of wetlands. Along the Atlantic Coast, tides are semidiurnal and symmetrical with a period of 12 hours and 25 minutes. In other words, there are roughly two high tides and two low tides each day. Since the tides are largely controlled by the position of moon relative to the sun, the highest and lowest tides (i.e., "spring tides") usually occur during full and new moons. Mean tidal ranges in Delaware Bay vary from 4.1 feet (1.25 m) at Cape Henlopen to 5.9 feet (1.80 m) at Woodland Beach (U.S. Department of Commerce 1978). Spring tidal ranges for these areas are 4.9 feet (1.49 m) and 6.8 feet (2.07 m), respectively. Along the Atlantic Ocean at Rehoboth Beach, the mean tidal range is 3.9 feet (1.19 m), whereas the spring tidal range is 4.7 feet (1.43 m). Coastal storms can also cause extreme high and low tides. Strong winds over a prolonged period have a great impact on the normal tidal range in large coastal bays.

In coastal wetlands, differences in hydrology (tidal flooding) create two zones that can be readily identified: (1) regularly flooded and (2) irregularly flooded (Figure 8). The regularly flooded zone is alternately flooded and

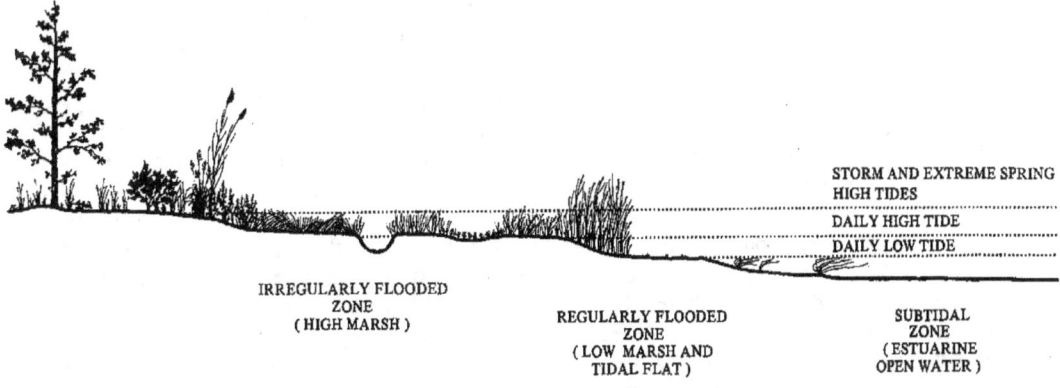

Figure 8. Hydrology of coastal wetlands showing different zones of flooding. The regularly flooded zone is flooded at least once daily by the tides, while the irregularly flooded zone is flooded less often.

exposed at least once daily by the tides. It includes both the "low marsh" and the more seaward intertidal mud and sand flats. Above the regularly flooded zone, the marsh is less frequently flooded by the tides, i.e., less often than daily. This irregularly flooded zone or "high marsh" is exposed to the air for long periods and flooded only for brief periods of variable length. The high marsh is usually flooded during spring tides. The upper margins of the high marsh may be flooded, however, only during storm tides which are more frequent in winter. Vegetative composition will vary with subtle differences in elevation and local drainage. Estuarine plants have adapted to these differences in hydrology and certain plants are generally good indicators of different water regimes (Table 9).

Table 9. Examples of plant indicators of the predominant tidal water regimes for Delaware's estuarine wetlands. These plants are generally good indicators of tidal flooding regimes.

Water Regime	Indicator Plants
Regularly flooded	Smooth Cordgrass (tall form)
	Spatterdock
	Pickerelweed
Irregularly flooded	Salt Hay Grass
	Spike Grass
	Smooth Cordgrass (short form)
	Black Grass
	Switchgrass
	Big Cordgrass

Some strictly freshwater wetlands are also subject to tidal flooding. They lie above the estuary where virtually no ocean-derived salts (i.e., less than 0.5 parts per thousand) are found. Here river flow and tidal flooding interact to create a rather complicated hydrology. Areas flooded and exposed at least once daily by the tides are considered regularly flooded as they are downstream in the estuary, yet wetlands that are not subject to daily tidal flooding are generally classified as seasonally flooded-tidal and temporarily flooded-tidal. They represent the more common water regimes in these situations, with the frequency and duration of flooding being the main hydrologic differences between them. Seasonally flooded-tidal wetlands are often flooded by tides and flooded waters may be present for long periods, especially during spring runoff. Temporarily flooded-tidal areas are flooded infrequently and when flooded, water does not usually persist for more than a few days. Freshwater tidal wetlands, especially forested wetlands, are quite similar in appearance to their nontidal counterparts, yet water levels are subject to tidal fluctuations.

Nontidal Wetland Hydrology

Beyond the influence of the tides, two hydrologic forces regulate water levels or soil saturation in wetlands: (1) surface water runoff and (2) ground-water discharge. Surface water runoff from the land either collects in depressional wetlands or overflows from rivers and lakes after snowmelt or rainfall periods (Figure 9). Ground water discharges into depressional wetlands where directly connected to the water table or into sloping wetlands in "seepage" areas (Figure 10). An individual wetland may exist due to surface water runoff or ground-water discharge or both. The role of hydrology in maintaining freshwater wetlands is discussed by Gosselink and Turner (1978).

Freshwater rivers and streams usually experience greatest flooding in winter and early spring, with maximum flooding occurring in March. Such flooding is associated with frozen soil, snow melt, and/or spring rains. In the summer, less water is available for runoff due to high evapotranspiration and to interception of rainfall by plant leaves. In the fall, the hurricane season normally brings heavy rains which increase flood heights and duration.

Water table fluctuations follow a similar pattern (Figure 11). From winter to mid-spring or early summer, the water table is at or near the surface in most wetlands. During this time, water may pond or flood the wetland surface for variable periods. In May or June, the water table begins to drop, reaching its low point in September or October. Most of the fluctuation relates to rainfall patterns, while longer days, increasing air temperatures, increasing evapotranspiration and other factors are responsible for the consistent lowering of the water table from spring through summer.

Standing water may be present in depressional, streamside or lakefront wetlands for variable periods during the growing season. When flooding or ponding is brief (usually 2 weeks or less), the wetland is considered temporarily flooded. During the summer, the water table may drop to 3 feet or more below the surface in these wetlands. This situation is prevalent along floodplains. Flooding for longer periods is described by three common water regimes: (1) seasonally flooded, (2) semipermanently flooded, and (3) permanently flooded. A seasonally flooded wetland typically has standing water visible for more than 1 month, but usually by late summer, this surface water is absent. If the water table remains at or very near the surface when not flooded or ponded, the water regime is considered seasonally flooded/saturated. By contrast, a semipermanently flooded wetland remains flooded

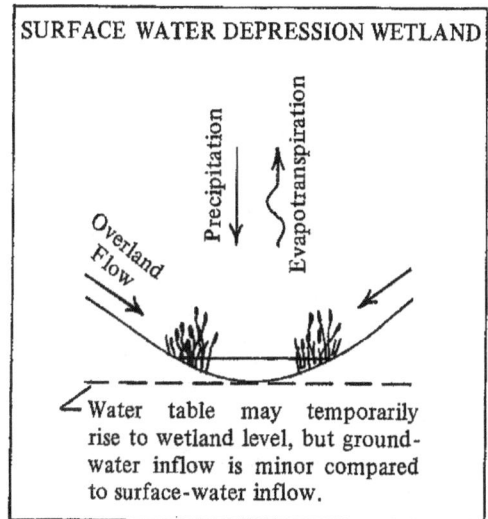

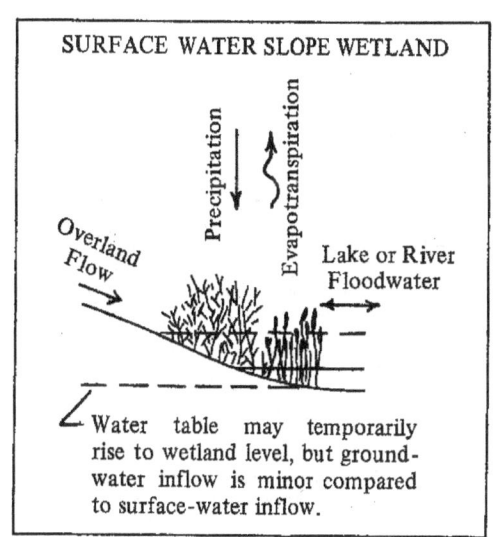

Figure 9. Hydrology of surface water wetlands (redrawn from Novitski 1982).

throughout the growing season in most years. Only during dry spells does the surface of these wetlands become exposed to air, yet the water table lies at or very near the surface. The wettest wetlands are permanently flooded, but they may be exposed during extreme droughts. These areas include open water bodies where the depth is less than 6.6 feet, e.g., ponds and shallow portions of lakes, rivers and streams.

Other wetlands are rarely flooded and are almost entirely influenced by ground-water discharge. These wetlands occur on considerable slopes in association with springs (i.e., points of active ground-water discharge), where they are commonly called "seeps". Their soils are saturated to the surface for most of the growing season and the water regime is, therefore, classified as saturated.

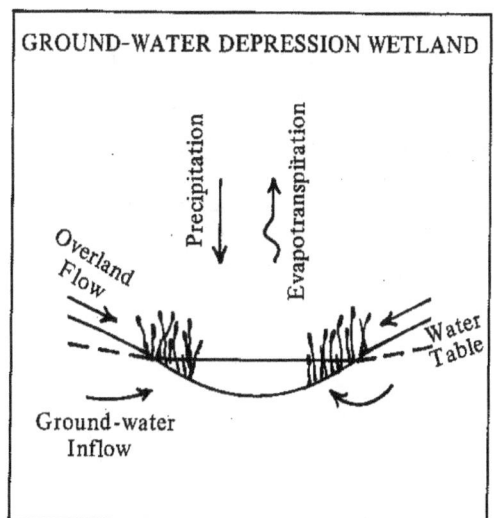

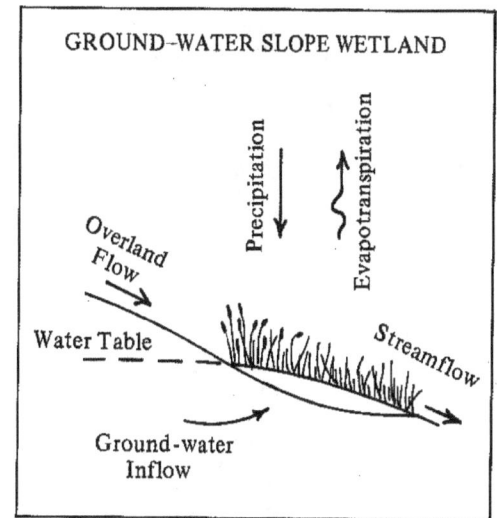

Figure 10. Hydrology of ground-water wetlands (redrawn from Novitski 1982).

26

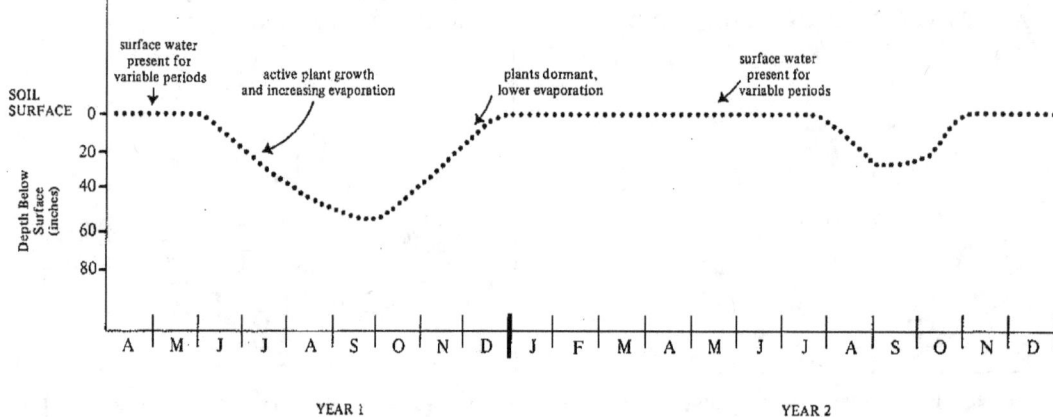

Figure 11. Water table fluctuations in a nontidal wetland (adapted from Lyford 1964). In general, the water table is at or near the surface through the winter and spring, drops markedly in summer, and begins to rise in the fall. As shown, the water table fluctuates seasonally and annually.

Common indicator plants of nontidal water regimes are presented in Table 10. Hydrologic conditions, e.g., water table fluctuation, flooding, and soil saturation, for each of Delaware's hydric soils are generally discussed in the following chapter. For more detailed information on wetland hydrology, the reader is referred to the following sources.

Table 10. Examples of plant indicators of the nontidal water regimes for Delaware's palustrine wetlands. These plants are generally useful indicators of certain water regimes.

Water Regime	Indicator Plants
Permanently flooded	Spatterdock
	White Water Lily
	Pondweeds
	Water Shield
Semipermanently flooded	Buttonbush
	Wild Rice
	Burreeds
	Pickerelweed
Seasonally flooded	Atlantic White Cedar
	Broad-leaved Cattail
	Tussock Sedge
	Skunk Cabbage
Temporarily flooded	Sycamore
	Beech
	American Holly
	Japanese Honeysuckle
	Partridgeberry

References

Carter, V., M.S. Bedinger, R.P. Novitski, and W.O. Wilen. 1979. Water resources and wetlands (Theme Paper). *In:* Greeson, P.E., J.R. Clark and J.E. Clark (editors). Wetland Functions and Values: The State of Our Understanding. American Water Resources Association, Minneapolis, Minnesota. pp. 344-376.

Cowardin, L.W., V. Carter, F.C. Golet, and E.T. LaRoe. 1979. Classification of Wetlands and Deepwater Habitats of the United States. U.S. Fish and Wildlife Service. FWS/OBS-79/31. 103 pp.

Gosselink, L.G. and R.E. Turner. 1978. The role of hydrology in freshwater wetland ecosystems. *In:* Good, R.E., D.F. Whigham, and R.L. Simpson (editors). Freshwater Wetlands. Ecological Processes and Management Potential. Academic Press, Inc., New York. pp. 63-78.

Leitch, J.A. 1981. Wetland Hydrology: State-of-the-Art and Annotated Bibliography. North Dakota State Univ., Agric. Expt. Stat. North Dakota Research Rept. No. 82. 16 pp.

Lyford, W.H. 1964. Water Table Fluctuations in Periodically Wet Soils of Central New England. Harvard University. Harvard Forest Paper No. 8. 15 pp.

Novitski, R.P. 1982. Hydrology of Wisconsin Wetlands. U.S. Geological Survey. Information Circular 40. 22 pp.

Sundstrom, R.W., T.E. Pickett, and R.D. Varrin. 1975. Hydrology, Geology and Mineral Resources of the Coastal Zone of Delaware. University of Delaware, Water Resources Center, Newark. Coastal Zone Management Program Tech. Rept. No. 3. 245 pp.

U.S. Department of Commerce. 1978. Tide Tables 1979. High and Low Water Predictions. NOAA, National Ocean Survey. 293 pp.

CHAPTER 5.

Hydric Soils of Delaware

Introduction

The predominance of undrained hydric soil is a key attribute for identifying wetlands (Cowardin, *et al.* 1979), although artificially created wetlands do exist on non-hydric soils. Hydric soils naturally develop in wet depressions, on floodplains, on seepage slopes, and along the margins of coastal and inland waters. Knowledge of hydric soils is particularly useful in distinguishing the drier wetlands from uplands, where the more typical wetland plants are less common or absent. This chapter focuses on Delaware's hydric soils, e.g., their characteristics, distribution and extent.

Definition of Hydric Soil

Hydric soils have been defined by the U.S.D.A. Soil Conservation Service (1982) as soil that is either: (1) saturated at or near the soil surface with water that is virtually lacking free oxygen for significant periods during the growing season, or (2) flooded frequently (i.e., more than 50 times in 100 years) for long periods (i.e., more than 7 consecutive days) during the growing season. This definition attempts to identify soils that support the growth and reproduction of hydrophytes or wetland vegetation. These soils are either saturated and/or flooded long enough to produce anaerobic (no oxygen) conditions in the soil, thereby affecting the reproduction, growth and survival of plants. Plants growing in wetlands must also deal with the presence of reduced forms of manganese, iron, and possibly sulfur, which are more toxic than their oxidized forms (Patrick 1983).

Soils that were formerly wet, but are now completely drained, are not considered hydric soils or wetlands according to the Service's wetland classification system (Cowardin, *et al.* 1979). These soils must be checked in the field to verify that drainage measures will remain functional under normal or design conditions. Where failure of drainage system results, such soils can revert to hydric conditions. This condition must be determined on a site-specific basis. Also excluded from the definition of hydric soils are soils that were not naturally wet, but are now subject to periodic flooding or soil saturation for specific management purposes (e.g., waterfowl impoundments) or flooded by accident (e.g., highway-created impoundments). Hydrophytic vegetation is usually present in these created wetlands. Moreover, well-drained soils that are frequently flooded for short intervals not long enough to support hydrophytes do not represent hydric soils.

The definition of hydric soil continues to be evaluated. Recently, the National Technical Committee for Hydric Soils was established for this purpose and to refine criteria and procedures for identifying hydric soils and to develop a single list of hydric soils for the country (W.B. Parker, pers. comm.). Their proposed definition follows: "A hydric soil is a soil that has, or has in its undrained condition, one or both of the following properties: (1) the soil is saturated at or near the soil surface with water that is virtually lacking free oxygen for a significant period during the growing season, and (2) the soil is frequently flooded or ponded for a long period during the growing season."

Major Categories of Hydric Soils

Hydric soils are separated into two major categories on the basis of soil composition: (1) organic soils (histosols) and (2) mineral soils. In general, soils having 20% or more organic material by weight in the upper 16 inches are considered organic soils, while soils with less organic content are mineral soils. For a technical definition, the reader is referred to **Soil Taxonomy** (U.S.D.A. Soil Conservation Service 1975).

Build-up of organic matter results from prolonged anaerobic soil conditions associated with long periods of flooding and/or soil saturation during the growing season. These saturated conditions impede aerobic decomposition (or oxidation) of the bulk organic materials, such as leaves, stems and roots, and encourage their accumulation as peat or muck over time. Consequently, most organic soils are characterized as very poorly drained soils. Organic soils typically form in water-logged depressions where peat or muck deposits range today from two feet to more than 30 feet in depth. They also develop in low-lying areas along coastal waters where tidal flooding is frequent. Organic soils can be further subdivided into three groups based on the percent of identifiable plant material in the soil: (1) muck (saprist) where two-thirds or more of the material is decomposed and less than one-third is identifiable, (2) peat (fibrist) with less than one-third decom-

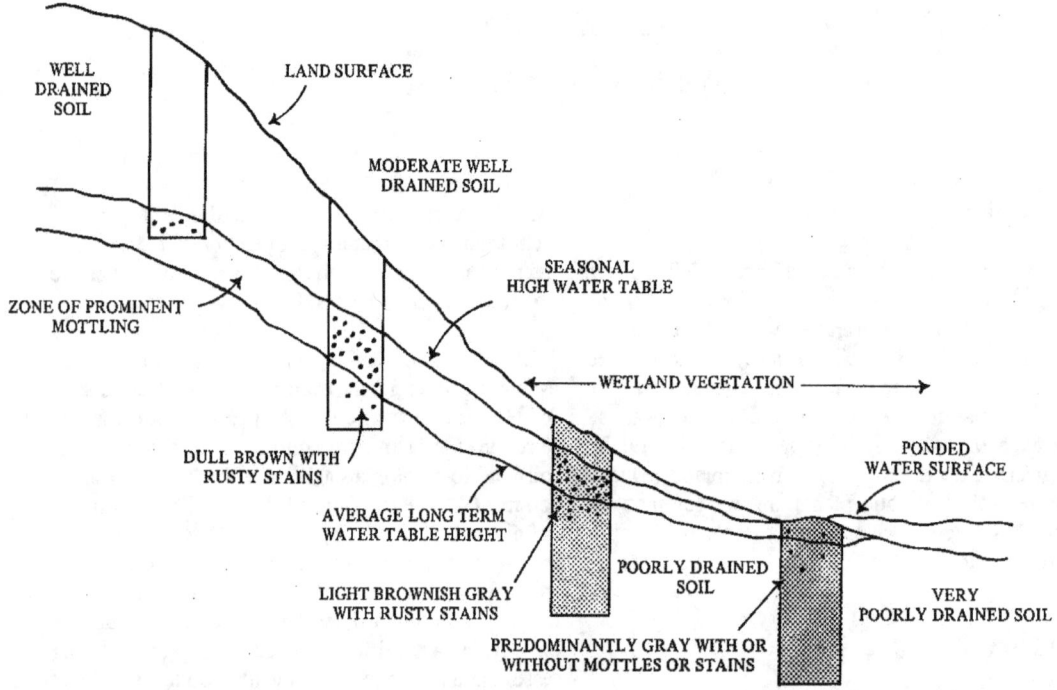

WELL DRAINED SOIL

LAND SURFACE

MODERATE WELL DRAINED SOIL

ZONE OF PROMINENT MOTTLING

SEASONAL HIGH WATER TABLE

WETLAND VEGETATION

DULL BROWN WITH RUSTY STAINS

AVERAGE LONG TERM WATER TABLE HEIGHT

PONDED WATER SURFACE

LIGHT BROWNISH GRAY WITH RUSTY STAINS

POORLY DRAINED SOIL

VERY POORLY DRAINED SOIL

PREDOMINANTLY GRAY WITH OR WITHOUT MOTTLES OR STAINS

Figure 12. Soil characteristics change from well-drained uplands to very poorly drained wetlands. Note that an increase in grayness of color is associated with increasing soil wetness (redrawn from U.S.D.A. Soil Conservation Service illustration).

posed and greater than two-thirds identifiable, and (3) mucky peat or peaty muck (hemist) where between one-third and two-thirds is both decomposed and identifiable. A fourth group of organic soils - folists - occur in boreal and tropical mountainous areas, but they do not develop under hydric conditions. All organic soils, with the exception of the folists, are hydric soils. For more information on organic soils, the reader is referred to **Histosols: Their Characteristics, Classification, and Use** (Aandahl, *et al.* 1974).

In many situations, organic matter does not accumulate in sufficient quantities to be classified as organic soils and here mineral soils have developed. Some mineral soils do, however, have thick organic surface layers related to excess soil moisture for long periods from heavy seasonal rainfall and/or a high water table (Ponnamperuma 1972). Mineral soils exhibit a wide range of properties related to differences in parent material, climate, topography, age, and other factors. Hydric mineral soils have standing water for significant periods and/or are saturated within 10 inches (25 cm) of the surface for extended periods during the growing season. Soil saturation may result from low-lying topographic position, ground-water seepage, or the presence of a slowly permeable layer (e.g., clay, confining bed, fragipan or hardpan). The duration and

depth of soil saturation are essential criteria for identifying hydric soils and wetlands. Soil morphology features are widely used to indicate long term soil moisture (Bouma 1983). The two most widely recognized features reflecting soil wetness are gleying and mottling. Gleyzation is the process of converting iron from its oxidized (ferric) form to its reduced (ferrous) state under prolonged periods of saturation (anaerobic conditions). Reduction and removal of reduced compounds result in gleying (Veneman, *et al.* 1975). Gleyed soils are typically bluish, greenish, or grayish in color and soils gleyed to or near the surface are hydric soils. Most soils that are alternately saturated and oxidized during the year are mottled (i.e., marked with spots or blotches of a different color or a different shade of the predominant soil matrix color) in the part of the soil that is wet. In most soils, depth and duration of saturation can be correlated to the quantity, nature, and pattern of soil mottling (Figure 12; Plate I). It is important, however, to note that mottles will not form during saturation under two conditions: (1) when the water contains sufficient oxygen to service microbial needs for digesting organic matter, and (2) when the soil or water temperatures are below biological zero (5 °C or 41 °F) during the time when the soil is saturated (Diers and Anderson 1984). Abundance, size, and color of the mottles usually indicate the length of saturation.

Mineral soils that are always saturated usually lack mottles and are uniformly gray throughout the saturated area. Mineral soils that are predominantly gray with brown or yellow mottles are usually saturated for long periods during the growing season, whereas soils that are predominantly brown or yellow with gray mottles are saturated for shorter periods, usually insufficient to be considered wetland. Soils that are never saturated are usually bright colored and are not mottled. In some hydric mineral soils, mottles may not be visible due to masking by organic matter (Parker, et al. 1984). While gleying and mottling are characteristic of nearly all hydric mineral soils, other soils with brighter colors may be saturated. This happens where the oxygen content of the soil remains high enough so that reduction of iron and manganese does not occur (Daniels, et al. 1973). In a study of Texas soils, Vepraskas and Wilding (1983) found that periods of saturation and reduction do not coincide; some soils were saturated for longer periods than they were reduced, while for other soils the reverse was true. Differences were related to water table recharge. Soils with a slowly permeable surface layer were not saturated throughout the upper soil even when they were ponded, but high moisture levels persisted and maintained reduced conditions for more than six months. The authors have proposed technical criteria for identifying these soils as hydric.

National List of Hydric Soils

To help the Service clarify its wetland definition, the U.S.D.A. Soil Conservation Service (SCS) agreed to develop a list of hydric soils. During formulation of this list, it became obvious that many soils exhibited some but not all of the common wetness characteristics and that the soils of the United States would be better grouped into three categories: hydric soils, soils with hydric conditions, and better drained soils that do not have hydric properties (Patrick 1983). Consequently, the SCS developed two national lists: (1) hydric soils and (2) soils with hydric conditions. The first list represents soils that are always associated with wetlands in their natural, undrained state. They almost always support hydrophytic vegetation. By contrast, the latter list contains soils that may under certain circumstances be coincident with wetlands. On-site field evaluations are needed to determine whether these soils support a predominance of hydrophytes. An examination of these two lists has suggested that the hydric soils list is conservative, while the list of soils with hydric conditions is too broad (Patrick 1983). Copies of these lists can be obtained from SCS's state office. In the future, the

National Technical Committee for Hydric Soils will publish an updated working list of hydric soils.

Delaware Hydric Soils

In Delaware, 15 soils have been identified as hydric soils (Table 11). Four land types mapped by the SCS also include wetlands, i.e., mixed alluvial land, muck, swamp and tidal marsh. Examples of three of Delaware's hydric soils and one non-hydric soil, for comparison, are shown on Plate I.

Table 11. List of Delaware's hydric soils and land types associated with wetlands.

Soil Series	Soil Series
Bayboro	Osier
Berryland	Othello
Calvert	Plummer
Elkton	Pocomoke
Fallsington	Portsmouth
Hatboro	Rutlege
Johnston	Watchung
Kinkora	

Land Types

Mixed Alluvial Land
Muck
Swamp
Tidal Marsh

Acreage of Hydric Soils

SCS soil mapping in Delaware identified 479,785 acres of hydric soils and land types associated with wetlands in the state. This represents nearly 38% of the state's land surface area. This figure may approximate Delaware's original wetland acreage, but does not represent the remaining acreage since the figure does not account for drainage, filling, impounding, and agricultural conversion of these wet soils.

The extent of hydric soils is related to the topography of the state, with the nearly level Coastal Plain area having more acreage than the rolling Piedmont region of northern Delaware. Consequently, Sussex County had the highest acreage of hydric soils and New Castle County the least. Acreages of each hydric soil found within each county are presented in Table 12.

Table 12. County summaries of hydric soils acreage in Delaware (taken from U.S.D.A. county soil surveys). Many acres of these soils have been drained and are no longer in a hydric condition.

County (Total Land Acreage)	Hydric Soil Type	Acres of Hydric Soil Types in County	% of County Covered by Hydric Soils
KENT (380,160)	Bayboro	645	
	Elkton	3,105	
	Fallsington	89,360	
	Johnston	9,315	
	Othello	10,140	
	Plummer	630	
	Pocomoke	30,950	
	Swamp	1,945	
	Tidal Marsh	38,995	
	Mixed Alluvial Land	1,010	
	Kent County Total =	186,095	= 49%
NEW CASTLE (280,320)	Bayboro	453	
	Calvert	(mapped with Watchung)	
	Elkton	9,745	
	Fallsington	26,192	
	Hatboro	3,398	
	Johnston	1,516	
	Kinkora	689	
	Mixed Alluvial Land	3,702	
	Othello	8,694	
	Pocomoke	1,161	
	Tidal Marsh	23,242	
	Watchung	2,368	
	New Castle County Total =	81,160	= 29%
SUSSEX (608,000)	Berryland	2,450	
	Elkton	3,560	
	Fallsington	82,200	
	Johnston	13,910	
	Muck	3,890	
	Osier	6,440	
	Pocomoke	65,030	
	Portsmouth	470	
	Rutlege	2,240	
	Swamp	5,960	
	Tidal Marsh	26,380	
	Sussex County Total =	212,530	= 35%

Description of Hydric Soils

This subsection briefly discusses key features of each hydric soil and land type associated with Delaware's wetlands. This information was obtained from published county soil surveys for Delaware and supplemented with hydrologic information from soil surveys from neighboring southern New Jersey.

Mixed Alluvial Land Type

Mixed alluvial land type is a mixture of soils that is too variable to map as a soil series unit. It ranges from well-drained soils to very poorly drained soils depending on site specific conditions. This type occurs along rivers and perennial streams. Alluvial areas are subjected to frequent flooding, most commonly in early spring. The water table is quite variable. In low areas, the water table is at the surface in winter and falls to one foot below in the summer. Ponding of water may be observed in places in late fall, winter and early spring due to the high water table. At higher levels, alluvial land may be only occasionally flooded, with the water table in winter two to three feet below the surface and in summer three or more feet below. Mixed alluvial land is mapped in Kent and New Castle Counties.

Plate I

Examples of three hydric soils and one non-hydric soil: (a) Berryland, (b) Pocomoke, (c) Fallsington, and (d) Evesboro (non-hydric). Note the following: Berryland soil has a 2 foot thick dark surface layer, underlain by an orange-colored sandy subsoil (the orange color represents iron oxide concretions and cemented layers resulting from a fluctuating water table); Pocomoke and Fallsington soils have a 1 foot thick dark surface layer and a gray layer mixed with bright colored mottles below (surface layer is darker in the Pocomoke soil and the water table is closer to the surface as evidenced by standing water at about 3 feet); Evesboro soil lacks hydric properties (e.g., thick dark surface layer and gray subsoil) near the surface and is more brightly colored than hydric soils.

Plate II

Plate III

a   Tiner

b   Zinni

Examples of Delaware's tidal wetlands: (a) salt marsh (estuarine), (b) brackish marsh (estuarine), (c) oligohaline marsh (estuarine), and (d) freshwater tidal marsh and shrub swamp (riverine and palustrine). Note: "cowlicks" in the salt hay grass marsh (a); tidal flooding in the brackish marsh; nonpersistent emergents along the creek in the oligohaline marsh; in (d) riverine tidal flat and nonpersistent emergent wetland in foreground and palustrine wetland of wild rice and shrubs in background.

c

Hardin

d

Tiner

Examples of Delaware's inland wetlands: (a) emergent wetland, (b) seasonally flooded forested wetland, (c) oak-dominated forested wetland, and (d) temporarily flooded loblolly pine wetland. Note: the larger dark area in (c) and smaller dark area in (d) represent wetter depressions within these wetlands.

c

Zinni

d

Zinni

Bayboro Series

The Bayboro series consists of very poorly drained, silty loams, with considerable clay in the subsoil. In depressions with no outlets, these soils are covered by water much of the winter and during wet periods. The water table remains at or near the surface until late spring. Bayboro soils are found in Kent and New Castle Counties.

Berryland Series

Berryland soils are very poorly drained, loamy sandy soils, with a hardpan in the subsoil (Plate I.a.). These soils usually occur on upland flats, in wide depressions and lowland flats and along streams. When bordering larger streams, these soils experience frequent flooding for short periods. During a normal rainfall year, these soils are saturated for seven to nine months. The water table reaches its peak in November with saturation to the surface and begins to drop in late May, attaining its lowest level (about two feet) by the end of July or August. Berryland soils are found in Sussex County.

Calvert Series

The Calvert series includes poorly drained soils occurring on upland flats and depressions in the Piedmont region of the state. They have a fragipan in the subsoil which keeps the soil wet for long periods. These soils are difficult to drain. Calvert soils are mapped as a complex with Watchung soils in New Castle County.

Elkton Series

The Elkton series consists of poorly drained, silty loamy or sandy loamy soils that have formed in former marine deposits. They occur in slight depressions on upland flats and low-lying areas. The water table is at the surface from fall through spring. Elkton soils are found in all three counties.

Fallsington Series

Fallsington soils are poorly drained, sandy loamy soils (Plate I.c.). They are found on large upland flats, in depressions and along streams where subjected to frequent flooding. These soils are generally saturated for six to eight months of the year (i.e., October to June) with the water table normally less than one foot. In summer, the water table drops to two feet or more. In winter, some areas may have water ponding on the surface. Fallsington soils are found in all three counties.

Hatboro Series

The Hatboro series include poorly drained, silty loamy soils occurring in the Piedmont region. They occur on floodplains and on uplands near the head of drains, along drainageways with no channels and at the foot of slopes. They are frequently flooded and have a seasonal high water table. Hatboro soils are found only in New Castle County.

Johnston Series

Johnston soils are very poorly drained, silty loamy soils of Coastal Plain floodplains. They have a high content of organic matter in their surface layers. In some areas, surface deposits of silty or sandy material are present. These soils are frequently flooded for variable periods and are wet for long periods. Johnston soils occur in all three counties.

Kinkora Series

The Kinkora series consists of poorly drained, silty loamy soils occurring on bench-like terraces above floodplains of major streams. These soils have poor natural drainage and a high water table. Kinkora soils are limited to the northern part of New Castle County.

Muck

The Muck land type is a very poorly drained to ponded, organic soil with a finely decomposed organic layer of about 14 to 23 inches lying over a loamy sand or sandy substratum. It occupies shallow, upland depressions. Muck is saturated ten to twelve months of the year, with the water table dropping in summer to one or two feet only during extreme droughts. Muck was mapped in Sussex County.

Osier Series

Osier soils consist of poorly drained, very sandy soils. They occur on upland flats and in depressions. They have poor natural drainage and a high seasonal water table that remains at or near the surface for very long periods. Water stands for long periods in depressions with no outlets. Osier soils are located in Sussex County.

Othello Series

The Othello series is composed of poorly drained, silty loamy soils. These soils occur on upland flats and adjacent to tidal marshes, where they are subjected to occasional flooding during severe coastal storms. The water table is at the surface or within one foot from late October to June and drops to three to five feet in summer. Othello soils are found in Kent and New Castle Counties.

Plummer Series

Plummer soils are poorly drained, loamy sandy soils. They are found on upland flats and in slight depressions. The water table is near the surface in winter, remains high in early spring and drops to four feet in summer. Plummer soils are restricted to Kent County.

Pocomoke Series

The Pocomoke series consists of very poorly drained, loamy and sandy loamy soils that have a high organic content at the surface (Plate I.b.). They occur in broad depressions and on upland flats. The water table is at the surface from October to May, dropping to two feet or more in summer, and rising again in September. Where located adjacent to streams, these soils are occasionally flooded. Pocomoke soils are located in all three counties.

Portsmouth Series

The Portsmouth series consists of very poorly drained, loamy soils that exist in shallow depressions and on upland flats. The water table is at the surface from winter through spring and falls only slightly to between one and two feet in summer. Portsmouth soils are limited to Sussex County.

Rutlege Series

Rutlege soils are very poorly drained, loamy sandy soils. They occur on upland flats and in depressions. Very poor natural drainage and a high seasonal water table characterize these soils. Rutlege soils are restricted to Sussex County.

Swamp

The Swamp land type consists of very poorly drained, organic soils. It occurs along streams, ponds and lakes and in low depressions with poor surface water drainage. These soils are saturated to the surface for at least ten months per year. This land type has been mapped in Kent and Sussex Counties.

Tidal Marsh

The Tidal Marsh land type consists of very poorly drained, silty or mucky flats that are associated with estuarine bays and tidal rivers. While they all lie near sea level in elevation, microtopography (i.e., small elevation changes) determines how frequently each area is flooded: daily or less often. These soils are almost continuously saturated. Tidal marsh soils are found in all three counties.

Watchung Series

The Watchung series includes poorly drained, silty loamy soils. These soils are found in depressions and on upland flats and gentle slopes. They are wet most of the year, with a seasonal high water table at or near the surface from late fall through early spring. Watchung soils are found in New Castle County and are often mapped as a complex with Calvert soils.

References

Aandahl, A.R., S.W. Buol, D.E. Hill, and H.H. Bailey (editors). 1974. Histosols: Their Characteristics, Classification, and Use. Soil Sci. Soc. Am. Special Pub. Series No. 6. 136 pp.

Bouma, J. 1983. Hydrology and soil genesis of soils with aquic moisture regimes. *In*: L.P. Wilding, N.E. Smeck, and G.F. Hall (editors). Pedogenesis and Soil Taxonomy I. Concepts and Interactions. Elsevier Science Publishers, B.V. Amsterdam. pp. 253-281.

Cowardin, L.M., V. Carter, F.C. Golet and E.T. LaRoe. 1979. Classification of Wetlands and Deepwater Habitats of the United States. U.S. Fish and Wildlife Service. FWS/OBS-79/31. 103 pp.

Daniels, R.B., E.E. Gamble, and S.W. Buol. 1973. Oxygen content in the groundwater of some North Carolina aquults and udults. *In*: R.R. Bruce, *et al.* (editors). Field Soil Water Regime. Soil Sci. Soc. Am., Madison, WI. pp. 153-166.

Delury, G.E. (editor) 1979. The World Almanac and Book of Facts 1979. Newspaper Enterprises Association, Inc. 976 pp.

Diers, R. and J.L. Anderson. 1984. Part I. Development of Soil Mottling. Soil Survey Horizons (Winter): 9-12.

Hole, T.J.F. and H.C. Smith. 1980. Soil Survey of Ocean County, New Jersey. U.S.D.A. Soil Conservation Service. 102 pp. and maps.

Ireland, W., Jr. and E.D. Matthews. 1974. Soil Survey of Sussex County, Delaware. U.S.D.A. Soil Conservation Service. 74 pp. and maps.

Johnson, J.H. 1978. Soil Survey of Atlantic County, New Jersey. U.S.D.A. Soil Conservation Service. 60 pp. and maps.

Markley, M. 1961. Soil Survey of Camden County, New Jersey. U.S.D.A. Soil Conservation Service. 94 pp. and maps.

Markley, M. 1962. Soil Survey of Gloucester County, New Jersey. U.S.D.A. Soil Conservation Service. 84 pp. and maps.

Markley, M.L. 1971. Soil Survey of Burlington County, New Jersey. U.S.D.A. Soil Conservation Service. 120 pp. and maps.

Markley, M.L. 1977. Soil Survey of Cape May County, New Jersey. U.S.D.A. Soil Conservation Service. 48 pp. and maps.

Matthews, E.D. and O.L. Lavoie. 1970. Soil Survey of New Castle County, Delaware. U.S.D.A. Soil Conservation Service. 97 pp. and maps.

Matthews, E.D. and W. Ireland, Jr. 1971. Soil Survey of Kent County, Delaware. U.S.D.A. Soil Conservation Service. 66 pp. and maps.

Parker, W.B., S. Faulkner, B. Gambrell, and W.H. Patrick, Jr. 1984. Soil wetness and aeration in relation to plant adaptation for selected hydric soils of the Mississippi and Pearl River Deltas. *In*: Proc. of Workshop on Characterization, Classification, and Utilization of Wetland Soils (March 26-April 24). Internat. Rice Res. Inst., Los Banos, Laguna, Philippines.

Patrick, W.H., Jr. 1983. Evaluation of Soil Conservation Service Hydric Soil Lists. Prepared for Waterways Expt. Station, U.S. Army Engineers, Vicksburg, MS. Contract No. DACW 39-82-M-2070. 13 pp. and appendices.

Ponnamperuma, F.N. 1972. The chemistry of submerged soils. Advances in Agronomy 24: 29-96.

Powley, V.R. 1969. Soil Survey of Salem County, New Jersey. U.S.D.A. Soil Conservation Service. 86 pp. and maps.

Powley, V.R. 1978. Soil Survey of Cumberland County, New Jersey. U.S.D.A. Soil Conservation Service. 69 pp. and maps.

U.S.D.A. Soil Conservation Service. 1975. Soil Taxonomy. U.S. Department of Agriculture. Agriculture Handbook No. 436. 754 pp.

U.S.D.A. Soil Conservation Service. 1982. Soils - Hydric Soils of the United States. U.S. Department of Agriculture. National Bulletin No. 430-2-7. (January 4, 1982).

U.S.D.A. Soil Conservation Service. 1983. Soils - List of Soils with Actual or High Potential for Hydric Conditions. U.S. Department of Agriculture. National Bulletin No. 430-3-10. (June 3, 1983). 28 pp.

Veneman, P.L.M., M.J. Vepraskas, and J. Bouma. 1976. The physical significance of soil mottling in a Wisconsin toposequence. Geoderma 15: 103-118.

Vepraskas, M.J. and L.P. Wilding. 1983. Aquic moisture regimes in soils with and without low chroma colors. Soil Sci. Soc. Am. J. 47: 280-285.

CHAPTER 6.

Vegetation and Plant Communities
of Delaware's Wetlands

Introduction

The vast majority of Delaware's wetlands are characterized by dense growths of plants adapted to existing hydrologic, water chemistry, and soil conditions, although some wetlands (e.g., tidal mudflats) are largely devoid of macrophytic plants. Most wetland definitions have relied heavily on dominant vegetation for identification and classification purposes. The presence of "hydrophytes" or wetland plants is one of the three key attributes of the Service's wetland definition (Cowardin, *et al.* 1979). Vegetation is usually the most conspicuous feature of wetlands and one that may be readily identified in the field. Other wetland characteristics, i.e., hydric soil and hydrology, may not be easily recognized and often require considerable scientific expertise, special training, or long-term study for accurate assessment. In this chapter, after discussing the concept of "hydrophyte," attention will focus on the major plant communities of Delaware's wetlands.

Hydrophyte Definition and Concept

Wetland plants are technically referred to as "hydrophytes." The Service defines a "hydrophyte" as "any plant growing in water or on a substrate that is at least periodically deficient in oxygen as a result of excessive water content" (Cowardin, *et al.* 1979). Thus, hydrophytes are not restricted to true aquatic plants growing in water, but also include plants morphologically and/or physiologically adapted to periodic flooding or saturated soil conditions of marshes, swamps, bogs and bottomland forests. Teskey and Hinckley (1977) have reviewed physiological responses and tolerance mechanisms of woody vegetation to flooding. The Service is preparing a comprehensive list of the Nation's hydrophytes to help clarify its wetland definition. This national list has been regionalized and a preliminary wetland plant list for the Northeast is available (U.S. Fish and Wildlife Service 1982). Final regional lists should be available by mid-1986.

The Service recognizes four types of hydrophytes: (1) obligate, (2) facultative wet, (3) facultative, and (4) facultative upland. Obligate hydrophytes are those plants which nearly always occur in wetlands (at least 99% of the time). The facultative types can be found in both wetlands and uplands to varying degrees. Facultative wet plants are usually associated with wetlands (from 66% to 99% of the time), while purely facultative hydrophytes show no affinity to wetlands or uplands and are found in wetlands with a frequency of occurrence between 33-66%. By contrast, facultative upland plants are seldom present in wetlands (less than 33% of the time). When present, they are usually in drier wetlands where they may even dominate or at higher elevations (e.g., hummocks) in wetter areas. In addition to these four types, the Service's list of hydrophytes also identifies drawdown plants that invade unvegetated wetlands (e.g., mudflats) during extreme dry periods. These plants are pioneer species with largely upland affinities. Examples of the four major types of hydrophytes for Delaware are presented in Table 13.

Wetland Plant Communities

Many factors influence wetland vegetation and community structure, including climate, hydrology, water chemistry, and human activities. Penfound (1952) identified the most important physical factors as: (1) location of the water table, (2) fluctuation of water levels, (3) soil type, (4) acidity, and (5) salinity. He also recognized the role of biotic factors, i.e., plant competition, animal actions, and human activities. Many construction projects alter the hydrology of wetlands through channelization and drainage or by changing surface water runoff patterns. These activities often have a profound effect on plant composition. This is particularly evident in Delaware's coastal marshes where mosquito ditching has increased the abundance of high-tide bush (*Iva frutescens*), especially on spoil mounds adjacent to ditches (Bourn and Cottam 1950). Repeated timber cutting and severe fires may also have profound effects on wetland communities.

Wetlands occur in Delaware in all five ecological systems inventoried by the NWI: Marine, Estuarine, Riverine, Lacustrine and Palustrine. In coastal areas, the estuarine marshes, which include salt and brackish tidal marshes and flats, are most abundant, with marine wetlands generally limited to intertidal beaches and bars at the mouths of tidal inlets in Sussex County. Overall, however, palustrine wetlands predominate, representing about 56% of the state's wetlands, whereas estuarine

Table 13. Examples of wetland plant types occurring in Delaware. Obligate plants are nearly always found in wetlands (at least 99% of the time); Facultative Wet plants are usually associated with wetlands (66-99% of the time); Facultative plants have no affinity to wetlands or uplands and are found in wetlands between 33-66% of the time; Facultative Upland plants are occasionally present in wetlands (less than 33% of the time).

Hydrophyte Type	Plant Common Name	Scientific Name
Obligate	Royal Fern	*Osmunda regalis*
	Pondweeds	*Potamogeton* spp.
	Smooth Cordgrass	*Spartina alterniflora*
	Cattails	*Typha* spp.
	Possumhaw	*Viburnum nudum*
	Swamp Azalea	*Rhododendron viscosum*
	Big Cranberry	*Vaccinium macrocarpon*
	Buttonbush	*Cephalanthus occidentalis*
	Atlantic White Cedar	*Chamaecyparis thyoides*
Facultative Wet	Cinnamon Fern	*Osmunda cinnamomea*
	Salt Hay Grass	*Spartina patens*
	Common Reed	*Phragmites australis*
	Inkberry	*Ilex glabra*
	Highbush Blueberry	*Vaccinium corymbosum*
	Basket Oak	*Quercus michauxii*
	Sycamore	*Platanus occidentalis*
Facultative	Foxtail Grass	*Setaria geniculata*
	Wrinkled Goldenrod	*Solidago rugosa*
	Purple Joe-Pye-weed	*Eupatoriadelphus purpureus*
	Sweet Pepperbush	*Clethra alnifolia*
	Sheep Laurel	*Kalmia angustifolia*
	Southern Arrowwood	*Viburnum dentatum*
	Red Maple	*Acer rubrum*
	Black Gum	*Nyssa sylvatica*
Facultative Upland	Bracken Fern	*Pteridium aquilinum*
	Partridgeberry	*Mitchella repens*
	Black Huckleberry	*Gaylussacia baccata*
	Beech	*Fagus grandifolia*
	American Holly	*Ilex opaca*
	White Ash	*Fraxinus americana*

wetlands represent 40%. Palustrine wetlands include the overwhelming majority of freshwater marshes, swamps, and ponds. Wetlands associated with the riverine and lacustrine systems are largely restricted to nonpersistent emergent wetlands, aquatic beds, and unvegetated flats. The following sections address major wetland types in each ecological system. Descriptions are based on field observations and a review of scientific literature. Nearly all of the literature relates to estuarine wetlands, with only little attention focused on palustrine wetlands. Fleming (1978) has generally described wetland communities for Delaware's outstanding natural areas.

Marine Wetlands

The Marine System includes the open ocean overlying the continental shelf and the associated coastline. Deep-water habitats predominate in this system, with wetlands generally limited to sandy intertidal beaches along the Atlantic Coast and bars at the mouths of coastal inlets. In Delaware, this system extends from the mouth of Delaware Bay and Cape Henlopen south to the Maryland border. Vegetation is sparse and scattered along with upper zones of beaches. Vascular plants like sea rocket (*Cakile edentula*), saltwort (*Salsola kali*), sandbur (*Cenchrus tribuloides*), beach grass (*Ammophila breviligulata*), beach orach (*Atriplex arenaria*), cocklebur (*Xanthium strumarium*), sea purslane (*Sesuvium maritimum*), and beach bean (*Strophostyles helvola*) occur in these areas (Silberhorn 1982).

Estuarine Wetlands

The Estuarine System consists of tidal brackish waters and contiguous wetlands where ocean water is at least occasionally diluted by freshwater runoff from the land. It extends upstream in coastal rivers to freshwater where no measurable ocean-derived salts (less than 0.5 parts per thousand) can be detected.

From a salinity standpoint, Delaware estuaries can be divided into three distinct reaches: (1) polyhaline - strongly saline areas (18-30 parts per thousand), (2) mesohaline (5-18 ppt), and (3) oligohaline - slightly brackish areas (0.5-5 ppt). Delaware Bay and large coastal rivers, such as the Indian and Leipsic Rivers, become increasingly fresher upstream from their mouths as saltwater becomes more diluted by freshwater runoff. A variety of wetland types develop in estuaries largely because of differences in salinity and duration and frequency of flooding. Major wetland types include: (1) intertidal flats, (2) emergent wetlands and (3) scrub-shrub wetlands. Estuarine wetlands are most extensive along Delaware Bay.

Estuarine Intertidal Flats

Intertidal flats of mud and/or sand are extremely common in estuaries, particularly between salt marshes and coastal bays. They are typically flooded by tides and exposed to air twice daily. These flats are generally devoid of macrophytes, although smooth cordgrass (*Spartina alterniflora*) may occur in isolated clumps.

Microscopic plants, especially diatoms, euglenoids, dinoflagellates and blue green algae, are often extremely abundant, yet inconspicous (Whitlatch 1982).

Estuarine Emergent Wetlands

Differences in salinity and tidal flooding within estuaries have a profound and visible effect on the distribution of emergent vegetation. Plant composition markedly changes from the more saline portions to the slightly brackish upstream areas. Even within areas of similar salinity, vegetation differs largely due to the frequency and duration of tidal flooding and locally to freshwater runoff. Examples of estuarine wetland plant communities are presented in Table 14 and shown on Plate II.

Salt Marshes

The more saline (polyhaline and mesohaline) reaches of estuaries are dominated by salt marshes (Plate II.a.). These estuarine wetlands are most widespread along

Table 14. Examples of estuarine wetland communities in Delaware.

Wetland Type (Halinity)	Dominance Type	Associated Plants	Water Regime
Emergent (polyhaline)	Smooth Cordgrass (tall form)	—	regularly flooded
Emergent (polyhaline)	Spike Grass and Black Grass	High-tide Bush, Big Cordgrass, Smooth Cordgrass (creekside), Salt Hay Grass, Seaside Goldenrod, and Sea Myrtle	irregularly flooded
Emergent (polyhaline)	Spike Grass	Salt Hay Grass, Common Three-square, High-tide Bush, Seaside Goldenrod, Big Cordgrass, Rose Mallow, Sea Myrtle, and Wax Myrtle	irregularly flooded
Scrub-Shrub (polyhaline)	High-tide Bush	Sea Lavender, Spike Grass, Salt Hay Grass, Common Reed, Wax Myrtle, and Poison Ivy	irregularly flooded
Emergent (mesohaline)	Switchgrass	Wax Myrtle, Sea Myrtle, Big Cordgrass, Red Cedar	irregularly flooded
Emergent (mesohaline)	Narrow-leaved Cattail, Rose Mallow, and Salt Hay Grass	Wax Myrtle, Sea Myrtle, Salt Marsh Bulrush, Switchgrass, Common Reed, Poison Ivy, and Red Cedar	irregularly flooded
Emergent (mesohaline)	Smooth Cordgrass (short form) and Salt Hay Grass	High-tide Bush, Marsh Orach, Big Cordgrass, Water Hemp, and Germander	irregularly flooded
Emergent (oligohaline)	Narrow-leaved Cattail and Rose Mallow	Common Reed and Smooth Cordgrass	irregularly flooded

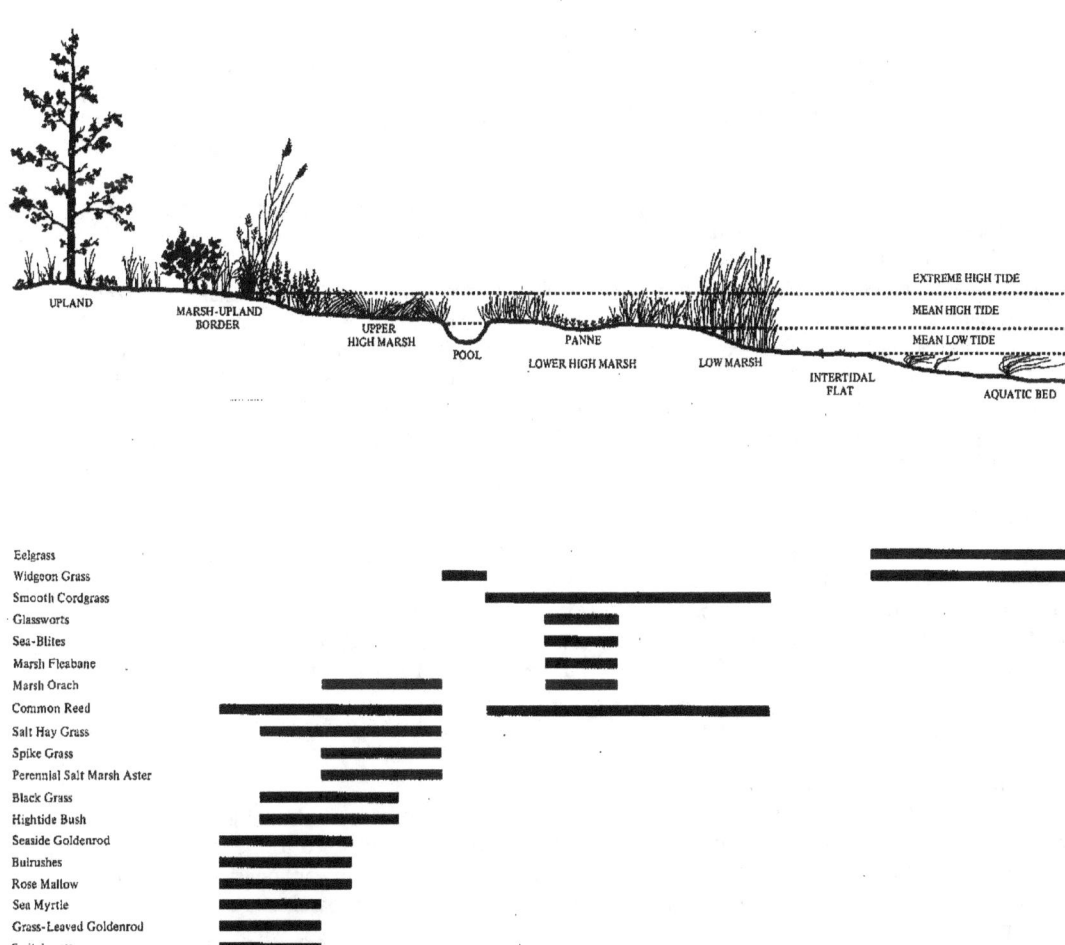

Figure 13. Generalized distribution of vegetation in Delaware's salt marshes. Note increased plant diversity along marsh-upland border. Also, common reed may be limited to the upper high marsh in many areas, but may also be prominent in the lower high marsh in other areas.

Delaware Bay, south of the Chesapeake and Delaware Canal to Lewes. A broad zonal pattern exists due to tidal flooding and two general zones are identified: (1) regularly flooded low marsh and (2) irregularly flooded high marsh (Figure 13).

The low marsh is flooded at least once daily by the tides. A tall form of smooth cordgrass (*Spartina alterniflora*) dominates this zone from approximately mean sea level to the mean high water mark. This zone is generally limited to creekbanks and upper borders or tidal flats. A recent study in Connecticut found that the tall form of smooth cordgrass was an accurate indicator of the landward extent of mean high tide

(Kennard, *et al.* 1983). According to state wildlife biologists, common reed (*Phragmites australis*) has displaced the tall form of smooth cordgrass from the low marsh in many locations.

Above this level is the high marsh which is flooded less often and is exposed to air for much greater periods. Vegetation here often forms a complex mosaic rather than a distinct zone. Plant diversity increases with several being abundant, including a short form of smooth cordgrass, salt hay grass (*Spartina patens*), spike grass (*Distichlis spicata*), glassworts (*Salicornia* spp.), marsh orach (*Atriplex patula*), sea lavender (*Limonium carolinianum*), salt marsh aster (*Aster tenuifolius*), black grass (*Juncus gerardii*), and common reed. Common reed and the short form of smooth cordgrass are particularly widespread high marsh plants. Pools and tidal creeks within the salt marshes may be vegetated with widgeon grass, sea lettuce, or other algae.

The short form of smooth cordgrass forms extensive stands just above the low marsh. Within these and higher areas, shallow depressions called pannes can be found. These pannes are subjected to extreme temperatures and salinity. Summer salinities may exceed 40 parts per thousand (Martin 1959). Although they may be devoid of plants, many pannes are colonized by a short form of smooth cordgrass and glassworts, while blue-green algae may form a dense surface mat.

Above the short cordgrass marsh, three grasses predominate: common reed, salt hay grass, and spike grass. Common reed forms either pure or mixed stands in the high marsh. Salt hay grass often forms nearly pure stands and is probably the more abundant of the latter two species, while spike grass is commonly intermixed. Spike grass commonly forms pure or nearly pure stands in the more poorly drained high marsh areas where standing water is present for extended periods. The short form of smooth cordgrass also frequently occurs in this zone. Black grass, which is actually a rush, is found at slightly higher levels often with high-tide bush (*Iva frutescens*). In the Little Assawoman Bay estuary, black needlerush (*Juncus roemerianus*) is locally common. This area represents the northern range limit of this species which is a dominant high marsh plant in Maryland, Virginia and further south. Ditches throughout the high marsh are immediately bordered by a tall or intermediate form of smooth cordgrass, while old spoil mounds adjacent to these mosquito ditches are vegetated by high-tide bush.

At the upland edge of salt marshes, switchgrass (*Panicum virgatum*), common reed, sea myrtle (*Baccharis halimifolia*), high-tide bush, wax myrtle (*Myrica cerifera*), and red cedar (*Juniperus virginiana*) may form the salt marsh border. Extensive fields of switchgrass frequently form the transition zone between upland and coastal wetland. Other plants present in border areas include bayberry (*Myrica pensylvanica*), poison ivy (*Toxicodendron radicans*), goldenrods (*Solidago sempervirens and Euthamia graminifolia*), foxtail grass (*Setaria geniculata*), and marsh pink (*Sabatia stellaris*). Where freshwater influence from the upland is strong, narrow-leaved cattail (*Typha angustifolia*), big cordgrass (*Spartina cynosuroides*), bulrushes (*Scirpus americanus and S. pungens*), marsh fern (*Thelypteris thelypteroides*), rose mallow (*Hibiscus*

moscheutos), and other brackish species may occur. Common three-square (*Scirpus pungens*) may form a border around forested and shrub hammocks within salt marshes. In many areas, salt marshes grade directly into fringing freshwater forested wetlands. Exposed and heavily weathered stumps of white cedars in salt marshes provide evidence of recent submergence of freshwater swamps by salt water.

Numerous scientific studies have been undertaken in Delaware's salt marshes. These studies are largely referenced by Daiber and others (1976). More recent studies have been completed by Dr. Franklin Daiber's students at the University of Delaware including Parker (1976), Tyrawski (1977), Clarke (1978), Phillips (1978), Jones (1978), Rennis (1978), Pennock (1981), Roman (1981), Simek (1981), Van House (1981), Watrud (1981), and Winkler (1981). In addition, Roman and Daiber (1984) have examined primary production dynamics in two Delaware tidal marshes. A detailed Fish and Wildlife Service report on New England high salt marshes (Nixon 1982) serves as a useful reference on the ecology of salt marshes.

Brackish Marshes

The brackish marshes in the middle (mesohaline) reach of estuaries are exposed to the widest ranges in salinity (5 to 18 ppt) which vary considerably between seasons. In spring, these marshes are mildly brackish due to heavy river discharge, while in late summer during low flows, salinity approaches that of the more saline marshes. From a vegetation standpoint, this area begins the large zone of transition where some of the common salt marsh plants, such as smooth cordgrass, salt hay grass, spike grass and switchgrass, first mix with freshwater species (Plate II.b.). This often gives the brackish marshes a more complex mosaic appearance than the salt marshes. Smooth cordgrass, salt hay grass, narrow-leaved cattail, big cordgrass, common reed, and rose mallow represent the major dominance types of the mesohaline marshes and they generally occupy the irregularly flooded areas. Smooth cordgrass and salt hay cordgrass are often intermixed with patches of big cordgrass and common reed (Roman and Daiber 1984). Rose mallow and cattail are often co-dominants, especially at more poorly drained locations often near the upland border. Plants in the regularly flooded zone may include salt and brackish species like smooth cordgrass and water hemp (*Amaranthus cannabinus*) as well as freshwater plants, e.g., arrow arum (*Peltandra virginica*), pickerelweed (*Pontederia cordata*), and soft-stemmed bulrush (*Scirpus validus*), in the more upstream brackish marshes. Arrow arum frequently occurs along riverbanks with cattails and big cordgrass in low salinity waters. Mesohaline marshes are associated with large tidal rivers, such as the Smyrna, Leipsic, St. Jones, Murderkill, Mispillion and Broadkill Rivers.

Oligohaline Marshes

Only traces of ocean-derived salts characterize the uppermost (oligohaline) estuarine marshes. They are predominantly freshwater influenced, with saltwater intrusion generally restricted to late summer and most evident within tidal channels. Oligohaline marshes may possess the highest diversity of all estuarine wetlands, since they lie between the strictly freshwater tidal marshes and the more brackish mesohaline wetlands. The regularly flooded zone is often dominated by non-persistent emergents, such as arrow arum, spatterdock (*Nuphar luteum*), arrowheads (*Sagittaria* spp.), or pickerelweed (Plate II.c.). In winter and early spring, this zone appears as an unvegetated mudflat. Smooth cordgrass can still be found along the banks in decreasing amounts. Big cordgrass, common reed, narrow-leaved cattail and rose mallow are common at high elevations. Sweet flag (*Acorus calamus*) and wild rice (*Zizania aquatica*) may be present in these wetlands, but are more abundant upstream in tidal freshwater areas. Other common plants include bulrushes (*Scirpus* spp.), sedges (*Carex* spp.), beggar-ticks (*Bidens* spp.), spikerushes (*Eleocharis* spp.), rushes (*Juncus* spp.), smartweeds (*Polygonum* spp.), and yellow flag (*Iris pseudacorus*). At the upper limits of the oligohaline reach, estuarine marshes are virtually indistinguishable from the strictly freshwater tidal marshes. Along this gradual transition, the main vegetation differences are the general absence of brackish plants like smooth cordgrass and the appearance of a dense shrub thicket border of wax myrtle and other woody plants. As the water becomes fresher, freshwater tidal swamps gradually form along the upland borders and become larger in size and move closer to the river with decreasing saltwater influence, eventually replacing shrub and emergent plant communities.

Estuarine Scrub-Shrub Wetlands

Estuarine shrub wetlands are not extensive along the Delaware coast, although some rather large stands exist. Where present, they are usually dominated by high-tide bush and sea myrtle. The former shrub is especially common along mosquito ditches in salt marshes where it has become established on mounds of deposited material. Both shrubs are common along upland edges

of salt marshes. Salt hay grass and spike grass are often co-dominants with high-tide bush, while big cordgrass, smooth cordgrass, rose mallow, and common reed are associated species (Daiber, *et al.* 1976). Black grass is sometimes present in stands of high-tide bush. Other common estuarine shrubs include northern bayberry and wax myrtle. These shrubs frequently grow along upland borders of salt marshes in association with switchgrass.

Riverine Wetlands

The Riverine System encompasses all of Delaware's freshwater rivers and their tributaries, including the freshwater tidal reaches of coastal rivers where salinity is less than 0.5 ppt. This system is generally dominated by deepwater habitats, with wetlands occurring between the river banks and deep water (6.6 feet and greater in depth). By definition, riverine wetlands are restricted to nonpersistent emergent wetlands, aquatic beds, and unvegetated shallow water or exposed areas. These wetlands are most extensive in tidal freshwater areas due to exposure of vast acreages of mudflats at low tide.

Riverine Tidal Wetlands

Riverine tidal wetlands consist mainly of intertidal mudflats and associated marshes of nonpersistent emergent plants (Plate II.d.). Contiguous freshwater tidal wetlands of persistent emergents, such as common reed and cattails, are classified as palustrine wetlands by Cowardin and others (1979). Both of these freshwater tidal wetlands are quite similar to the oligohaline marshes immediately downstream. The dominant riverine emergents are sweet flag, arrow arum, wild rice, pickerelweed, and spatterdock. Other common plants include smartweeds, beggar-ticks, jewelweed (*Impatiens capensis*), burreeds (*Sparganium* spp.), arrowheads (*Sagittaria latifolia* and others), and water hemp. These plants are present in the regularly flooded zones and many intermix with persistent emergents forming large stands of palustrine tidal wetlands in the irregularly flooded areas. Tussock-sedge (*Carex stricta*), a persistent emergent, occurs in scattered clumps in these regularly flooded wetlands to a lesser extent.

Vegetation is not always evident in these marshes due to the predominance of nonpersistent emergents. By definition, these nonpersistent plants readily decompose after the growing season and their remains are not found standing in the marshes in spring. Tidal riverine emergent wetlands, therefore, appear as mudflats during low tide in the winter and early spring. During the growing season, the visual picture or physiognomy of these wetlands changes dramatically. In late spring and early summer, sweet flag and broad-leaved emergents, particularly spatterdock, arrow arum and pickerelweed, dominate, since their leaves are among the first to emerge. As the season progresses, taller growing plants like water hemp, wild rice, smartweeds, and beggar-ticks become visually dominant.

Riverine Nontidal Wetlands

Although many of the state's freshwater wetlands lie along nontidal rivers and streams, only a small fraction of these are considered riverine wetlands according to the Service's classification system (Cowardin, *et al.* 1979). Riverine wetlands are by definition largely restricted to aquatic beds within the channels and to fringes of nonpersisent emergent plants growing on river banks or in shallow water. Contiguous wetlands dominated by persistent vegetation (i.e., trees, shrubs, and robust emergents) are classified as palustrine wetlands.

Nontidal riverine wetlands are most visible along slow-flowing, meandering lower perennial rivers. Here nonpersistent emergent plants like burreeds, pickerelweed, arrowheads, arrow arum, rice cutgrass (*Leersia oryzoides*), and smartweeds may colonize very shallow waters and exposed shores. Aquatic beds may also become established in slightly deeper waters of clear rivers and streams. Important aquatic bed plants include submerged forms of burreeds and arrowheads, pondweeds and riverweeds (*Potamogeton* spp.), spatterdock and white water lily (*Nymphaea odorata*).

Palustrine Wetlands

The majority of Delaware's wetlands, i.e., freshwater marshes, swamps and bottomland forests, are classified as palustrine wetlands. They represent the most floristically diverse group of wetlands in the state. This collection of wetlands is subjected to a wider range of water regimes than wetlands of other systems, with the more common water regimes being permanently flooded, semipermanently flooded, seasonally flooded, and temporarily flooded. Certain tidally influenced freshwater areas are also considered palustrine wetlands. While numerous plants may be restricted to one or two sets of hydrologic regimes, many plants like red maple (*Acer rubrum*) and purple loosestrife (*Lythrum salicaria*) tolerate a wide range of flooding and soil saturation conditions. Although their tolerances may be high, wetland plants are usually more prevalent under certain

water regimes and may, therefore, be used as good indicators of certain flooding and soil saturation conditions. Examples of plant-water regime relationships are presented in Table 10 (Chapter 4). Palustrine wetland plant communities are discussed by class in the following subsections and examples are shown on Plate III. The reader must recognize the diversity of these communities and that this discussion attempts to characterize the major types in general terms.

Palustrine Aquatic Beds

Artificially-created ponds are common throughout the state. These permanently flooded water bodies comprise the wettest of palustrine wetlands. Many shallow ponds have aquatic beds covering all or part of their surfaces or bottoms. Common dominance types include green algae, floating species like duckweeds (*Lemna* spp. and others), and rooted vascular plants, such as spatterdock, white water lily, water shield (*Brasenia schreberi*), mermaidweed (*Proserpinaca palustris*), and pondweeds.

Palustrine Emergent Wetlands

Palustrine emergent wetlands are freshwater marshes dominated by persistent and nonpersistent grasses, rushes, sedges, and other herbaceous or grass-like plants. In general, they can be divided into two groups based on hydrology: (1) tidal emergent wetlands, and (2) nontidal emergent wetlands.

Along tidal freshwater rivers and lying generally above the mean high tide mark, wetlands of persistent vegetation commonly occur. These emergent wetlands fall within the Palustrine System due to the predominance of persistent vegetation, whereas adjacent marshes of nonpersistent emergents are part of the Riverine System according to the Service's wetland classification system (Figure 14; Cowardin, *et al.* 1979). Palustrine tidal emergent wetlands are commonly represented by a mixed plant community of narrow-leaved cattail and rose mallow or by other common emergents including beggar-ticks (*Bidens laevis* and others), yellow flag, water smartweed (*Polygonum punctatum*), tearthumbs (*Polygonum arifolium* and *P. sagittatum*), wild rice, broad-leaved arrowhead (*Sagittaria latifolia*), water hemp, arrow arum, common reed, pickerelweed, water willow (*Decodon verticillatus*), river bulrush (*Scirpus fluviatilis*), jewelweed, sweet flag, soft-stemmed bulrush, marsh fern, blue flag (*Iris versicolor*), soft rush (*Juncus effusus*), and broad-leaved cattail. Often associated with these tidal emergent wetlands are scat-

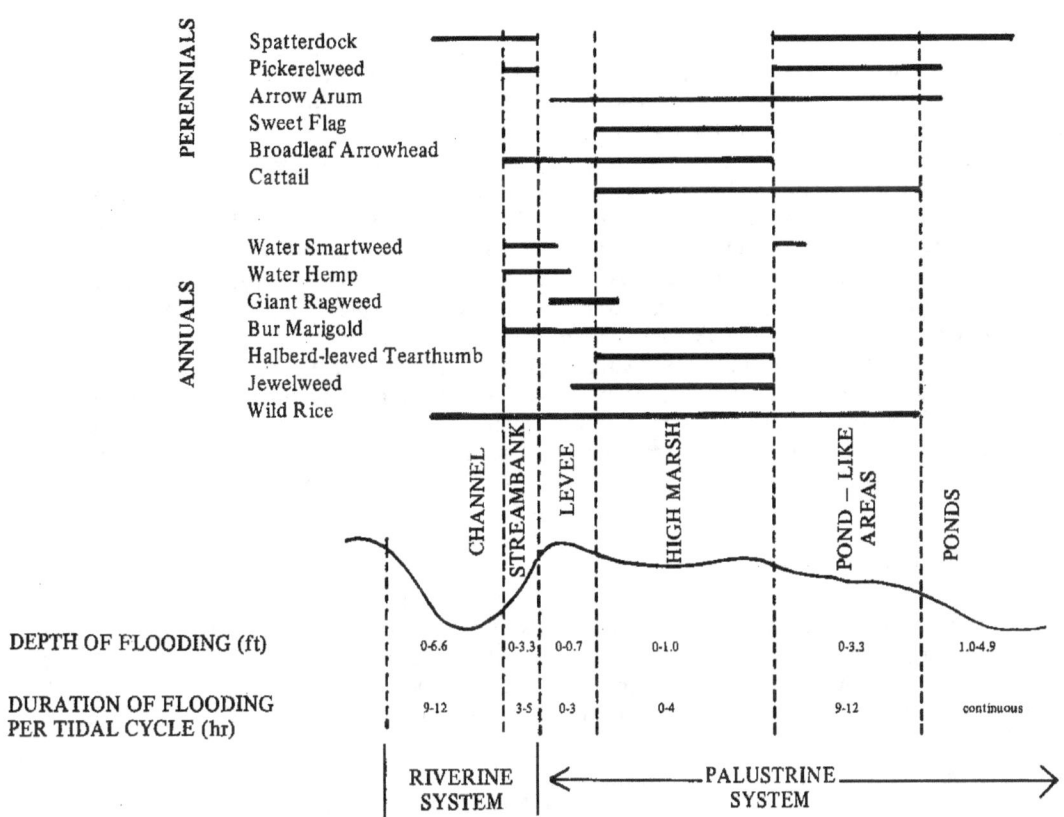

Figure 14. Generalized plant zonation in a freshwater tidal wetland from neighboring New Jersey (adapted from Simpson, *et al.* 1983). Note that wetland vegetation occurs in two systems - Riverine and Palustrine. Plant distribution in Delaware may differ slightly, e.g., sweet flag has been observed on streambanks.

tered shrubs and trees, such as willows (*Salix* spp.), buttonbush (*Cephalanthus occidentalis*), swamp rose (*Rosa palustris*), red maple, and wax myrtle.

Freshwater emergent wetlands beyond tidal influence are common throughout the state, being about four times more abundant than the palustrine tidal marshes. Compared to the palustrine forested wetlands, however, these emergent wetlands represent only a small portion of the state's freshwater wetlands.

Freshwater marshes are subjected to a variety of water regimes which affect plant community composition. Semipermanently flooded emergent marshes may be dominated by broad-leaved cattail (*Typha latifolia*), spatterdock, arrow arum, water willow, and burreed, while spikerushes may dominate these marshes during drawdown or drought conditions. Associated plants include duckweeds, rose mallow, pickerelweed, yellow flag, and blue flag. Dominant emergents of seasonally flooded areas include rice cutgrass, broad-leaved cattail, narrow-leaved cattail, soft rush, reed canary grass

(*Phalaris arundinacea*), sweet flag, arrow arum, sedges, and willow herb (*Epilobium* spp.) (Plate III.a.). Other common plants are jewelweed, tearthumbs, meadow beauties (*Rhexia* spp.), common reed, smartweeds, sensitive fern (*Onoclea sensibilis*), marsh fern, woolgrass (*Scirpus cyperinus*), beakrushes (*Rhynchospora* spp.), boneset (*Eupatorium perfoliatum*), asters, broad-leaved arrowhead, spikerushes, and Joe-Pye-weeds (*Eupatorium* spp. and *Eupatoriadelphus* spp.). Less common emergents in seasonally flooded marshes include bedstraw (*Galium tinctorium*), common three-square, swamp dock (*Rumex verticillatus*), dodder (*Cuscuta gronovii*), swamp milkweed (*Asclepias incarnata*), skunk cabbage (*Symplocarpus foetidus*), and panic grasses (*Panicum* spp. and *Dichanthelium* spp.). Shrubs, such as willows, buttonbush, swamp rose, elderberry (*Sambucus canadensis*), smooth alder (*Alnus serrulata*), and silky dogwood (*Cornus amomum*), and saplings of red maple may be scattered within these wetlands. Temporarily flooded emergent wetlands may be dominated by soft rush, reed canary grass, common reed, goldenrods (*Solidago* spp. and *Euthamia* spp.),

Joe-Pye-weeds, asters, and others. Pothole-type emergent wetlands in Kent and New Castle Counties are probably similar to those reported on the Eastern Shore of Maryland by Sipple (1977). Dominant emergents may include: plume grass (*Erianthus giganteus*), sedge (*Carex rostrata* and *C. walteriana*), and twigrush (*Cladium mariscoides*). Peat moss (*Sphagnum* spp.) forms a dense groundcover, while clumps of persimmon (*Diospyros virginiana*) may be present in these pothole wetlands. Certain palustrine emergent wetlands contain numerous rare plants. Two wetlands in the Ellendale area (the New Market Wetland and the Ellendale Wet Meadow) are the only known sites for many of Delaware's rare plants according to the Division of Parks and Recreation, Office of Nature Preserves.

Palustrine Scrub-Shrub Wetlands

Although not as abundant as palustrine forested and emergent wetlands, scrub-shrub wetlands are not uncommon throughout the state. They are characterized by the dominance of shrubs or tree saplings less than 20 feet (6 m) in height. They exist in both tidal and nontidal environments.

Palustrine scrub-shrub wetlands are conspicuous along tidal rivers, such as Spring Creek, Murderkill River, St. Jones River, Cedar Creek, and Broadkill River. These wetlands are extremely wet due to frequent tidal flooding. The plant communities, while dominated by two species (wax myrtle and red maple), are quite diverse. Other common shrubs contributing to this dense wet thicket are poison ivy, winterberry (*Ilex verticillata*), swamp rose, and red chokeberry (*Aronia arbutifolia*). Poison ivy was abundant and observed growing upright to a height of 8 feet along Spring Creek. Other associated vegetation includes buttonbush, highbush blueberry (*Vaccinium corymbosum*), sweet pepperbush (*Clethra alnifolia*), smooth alder, seaside alder (*Alnus maritima*), sea myrtle, sweet bay (*Magnolia virginiana*), southern wild raisin (*Viburnum nudum*), southern arrowwood (*Viburnum dentatum*), elderberry, swamp azalea (*Rhododendron viscosum*), maleberry (*Lyonia ligustrina*), greenbriar (*Smilax rotundifolia*), rose mallow, tussock and other sedges, narrow-leaved cattail, jewelweed, water parsnip (*Sium suave*), arrow arum, tearthumbs, bugleweed (*Lycopus virginicus*), blue flag, marsh violet (*Viola cucullata*), soft rush, swamp milkweed, royal fern (*Osmunda regalis*), cinnamon fern (*Osmunda cinnamomea*), and climbing hempweed (*Mikania scandens*).

In nontidal areas, shrub wetland dominants include true shrubs of buttonbush, silky dogwood, and smooth alder and saplings of red maple, ashes (*Fraxinus* spp.) and black willow. Buttonbush is most abundant in semipermanently flooded wetlands, while other woody plants are more common in seasonally flooded and drier wetlands. Buttonbush may be associated with water willow, broad-leaved cattail, and persimmon, particularly in pothole wetlands in Kent and New Castle Counties. Sipple (1977) found water willow and buttonbush as co-dominants in neighboring Maryland counties. He also observed mixed emergent and shrub pothole wetlands where buttonbush was mixed with plume grass, sedges, bald rush (*Psilocarya scirpoides*), fimbristylis (*Fimbristylis autumnalis*), St. John's-worts (*Hypericum* spp.), and other plants. Seaside alder, Virginia sweetspire (*Itea virginica*), swamp rose, water willow, red maple, and Atlantic white cedar (*Chamaecyparis thyoides*) saplings were observed in a mixed scrub-shrub wetland in Sussex County. In many seasonally flooded scrub-shrub wetlands, plants associated with the dominant species include broad-leaved cattail, rice cutgrass, woolgrass, smartweeds, skunk cabbage, jewelweed, dodder, sedges, soft rush, sensitive fern, and various mosses.

Palustrine Forested Wetlands

Palustrine forested wetlands represent the most abundant and widely distributed wetland type in the state. Most swamps lie along rivers and streams or in upland depressions, yet some border salt marshes along the coast. Forested wetlands are characterized by the dominance of woody plants taller than 20 feet (6 m). These wetlands occur in freshwater areas in both tidal and nontidal situations.

Tidally-influenced forested wetlands are common along the upper reaches of tidal rivers, such as the Nanticoke, Mispillion, and Murderkill Rivers (Figure 15). Deciduous trees predominate, with green ash (*Fraxinus pennsylvanica* var. *subintegerrima*), red maple, and black gum being most abundant. In some areas, green ash appears to dominate areas closer to the river, while red maple becomes more abundant away from the water. In other cases, red maple dominates the entire wetland. Black willow and sweet bay are also common, while American holly (*Ilex opaca*) and sweet gum are less common. Needle-leaved evergreen trees, i.e., Atlantic white cedar and loblolly pine (*Pinus taeda*), are also present in smaller amounts, although white cedar may be locally dominant. Common shrubs forming a dense shrub understory include southern arrowwood, sweet pepperbush, highbush blueberry, swamp azalea, smooth alder, winterberry, and

Figure 15. Freshwater tidal wetlands along the Nanticoke River: riverine tidal emergent wetland along water's edge, with seasonally flooded-tidal palustrine forested wetland behind.

spicebush (*Lindera benzoin*). Other important, but usually less abundant shrubs, are maleberry, fetterbush (*Leucothoe racemosa*), elderberry, silky dogwood, swamp rose, wax myrtle, southern wild raisin, seaside alder, and Virginia sweetspire. Greenbriars (*Smilax* spp.), grape (*Vitis* spp.), and poison ivy are common vines. Emergent vegetation may be common in relatively open canopies with arrow arum, tussock sedge and other sedges, soft rush, royal fern, cinnamon fern, violet (*Viola* spp.), jewelweed, lizard's-tail (*Saururus cernuus*), halberd-leaved tearthumb (*Polygonum arifolium*), beggar-ticks, bugleweed, skunk cabbage, jack-in-the-pulpit (*Arisaema triphyllum*), and tall meadow rue (*Thalictrum pubescens*) observed. Wild rice may occur along the waterward edges of tidal swamps. American mistletoe (*Phoradendron flavescens*) may be present in trees, especially red maple and black gum.

Nontidal forested wetlands are the predominant wetland type in Delaware. Both deciduous and evergreen forested wetlands occur with the former being over seven times more abundant. These wetlands, like other freshwater wetlands, are exposed to a wide array of water regimes, ranging from permanently flooded to temporarily flooded.

Permanently flooded forested wetlands are extremely rare in the state and where present, they are dominated by bald cypress (*Taxodium distichum*) which is at the northern limit of its geographical range. An example of this wetland type can be seen at Trussum Pond in Sussex County (Figure 16). A dam has impounded waters in this area for at least 100 years (Fleming 1978). Here, bald cypress is associated with white water lily, spatterdock, pickerelweed, burreed, pondweeds, and other plants. At the southeastern end of nearby Trap Pond, bald cypress dominates a semipermanently flooded wetland. This wetland grades into a seasonally flooded forested wetland

where bald cypress is co-dominant with red maple and black gum. Common associates here include green ash, smooth alder, sweet pepperbush, and lizard's-tail. Along James Branch, bald cypress dominates seasonally flooded forested wetlands, with other trees (e.g., loblolly pine, sweet gum, and red maple) also forming part of the canopy (Fleming 1978). Understory trees and shrubs include American holly, sweet bay, southern arrowwood, and strawberry-bush (*Euonymus americanus*). Other plants present are poison ivy, sand blackberry (*Rubus cuneifolius*), net-veined chain fern (*Woodwardia areolata*), and oblique grape fern (*Botrychium dissectum*).

Red maple is the most widespread tree in Delaware's forested wetlands. It usually dominates seasonally flooded swamps and is very abundant and often predominant in temporarily flooded areas as well. Other trees dominating seasonally flooded swamps include sweet gum, various oaks, Atlantic white cedar, and loblolly pine.

Red maple swamps are the most common wetland type throughout the state. In seasonally flooded situations, it is often the sole dominant tree species, although occasionally sweet gum, black gum, or loblolly pine occur in large numbers as co-dominants (Plate III.b.). Other associated trees are ashes, river birch (*Betula nigra*), sweet bay, basket oak (*Quercus michauxii*), swamp white oak (*Q. bicolor*), pin oak (*Q. palustris*), and American elm (*Ulmus americanus*). In certain areas, various oaks dominate seasonally flooded wetlands (Plate III.c.). In drier situations and at higher elevations in wet swamps, black cherry (*Prunus serotina*), tulip tree (*Liriodendron tulipifera*), willow oak (*Quercus phellos*), beech (*Fagus grandifolia*), red oak (*Quercus rubra*), and American holly may be present. Shrubs forming a thicket understory in seasonally flooded red maple swamps include sweet pepperbush, southern arrowwood, winterberry, highbush blueberry, maleberry, fetterbush, Virginia sweetspire, and swamp

Figure 16. Bald cypress in Trussum Pond.

azalea. Poison ivy, greenbriar, and Japanese honeysuckle (*Lonicera japonica*) usually become quite common in drier (temporarily flooded) red maple swamps. Common herbaceous plants of wetter swamps consist of skunk cabbage, royal fern, cinnamon fern, sensitive fern, net-veined chain fern, lizard's-tail, tussock sedge and other sedges, jewelweed, jack-in-the-pulpit, tall meadow rue, and others. Peat moss may be locally abundant in wetter depressions, while water willow may be common in wet open areas. Canada mayflower (*Maianthemum canadense*) and trout lily (*Erythronium umbilicatum*) may occur on hummocks. Examples of the variety of plant composition within red maple-dominated wetlands are presented in Table 15.

Temporarily flooded deciduous forested wetlands are the most abundant forested wetland type in Delaware. Many of them represent once wetter swamps that have now been partly drained by channelization projects.

Several tree species may dominate or share the forest canopy, including red maple, sweet gum, tulip tree, green ash, white ash (*Fraxinus americana*), black gum, oaks (e.g., pin, red, swamp white, and willow), loblolly pine, and American elm. In the Piedmont region, box elder (*Acer negundo*), sycamore (*Platanus occidentalis*), ironwood (*Carpinus caroliniana*), beech, silver maple (*Acer saccharinum*), bitternut (*Carya cordiformis*), spicebush, stinging nettle (*Urtica dioica*), spring beauty (*Claytonia virginica*), and may apple (*Podophyllum peltatum*) may be present and even locally abundant. In the Coastal Plain region, loblolly pine, American holly, sweet pepperbush, inkberry (*Ilex glabra*), elderberry, and highbush blueberry are more typical plants. Poison ivy, greenbriar, and Japanese honeysuckle are common in many temporarily flooded swamps, with partridgeberry (*Mitchella repens*) occurring in lesser amounts. Hercules club (*Aralia spinosa*) is occasionally present in these wetlands in Sussex

Table 15. Examples of red maple forested wetland communities in Delaware.

Dominance Type (Water Regime)	Common Associates	Less Common Plants
Red Maple (seasonally flooded/saturated)	Black Gum, Sweet Gum, Basket Oak, Sedges, and Winterberry	American Elm, American Holly, Lizard's-tail, Greenbriar, Grape, Southern Arrowwood, Trumpet Creeper, and Beggar-ticks
Red Maple (seasonally flooded/(saturated)	Sweet Pepperbush and Mosses	Sweet Gum, Highbush Blueberry, Swamp Azalea, Southern Arrowwood, and Black Gum
Red Maple (seasonally flooded/saturated)	Southern Arrowwood, Skunk Cabbage, Sensitive Fern, Net-veined Chain Fern, and Manna Grass	Sweet Bay
Red Maple (seasonally flooded)	Elderberry, Jack-in-the-pulpit, Jewelweed, Poison Ivy, and Grass	Marsh Blue Violet, Small-flowered Crowfoot, Skunk Cabbage, Silky Dogwood, Smartweed, Elm, and Greenbriar
Red Maple (seasonally flooded)	Silky Dogwood, Skunk Cabbage, Sensitive Fern, and Southern Arrowwood	Pin Oak, False Nettle, Soft Rush, Poison Ivy, Sedges, Grasses, Elderberry, Grape, Bitter Cress, and Sweet Gum
Red Maple (seasonally flooded)	Swamp Rose, St. John's-wort, Peat Moss, other Mosses, and Meadowsweet	Highbush Blueberry, Loblolly Pine (seedlings), and Dogbane
Red Maple, Sweet Gum and Loblolly Pine (temporarily flooded)	American Holly, Sweet Bay, Greenbriar, Highbush Blueberry, Poison Ivy, and Brambles	Choke Cherry, Inkberry, Sweet Pepperbush, Ironwood, Beech, Water Oak, and Clubmoss
Red Maple (temporarily flooded)	Black Gum and Poison Ivy	Sweet Gum, Willow Oak, Peat Moss, Soft Rush, Sedges, Greenbriar, Highbush Blueberry, and Pin Oak
Red Maple, Bitternut and Sweet Gum (temporarily flooded)	Sweet Pepperbush, Highbush Blueberry, and Greenbriar	Willow Oak, Swamp White Oak, Pin Oak, Southern Arrowwood, Grass and Sedges

Table 16. Examples of temporarily flooded forested wetland communities in Delaware.

Dominance Type	Common Associates	Less Common Vegetation
Tulip Tree and Ash	Ironwood, Spring Beauty, Japanese Honeysuckle, and Spicebush	May Apple, Poison Ivy, Violet, Jack-in-pulpit, Trout Lily, Wild Garlic, Skunk Cabbage, Silky Dogwood, Black Cherry, Brambles, Elderberry, Greenbriar, and Jewelweed
American Elm and Red Maple	Sycamore, Jewelweed, Stinging Nettle, and Spicebush	Bluebells, May Apple, Spring Beauty, Silver Maple, Elderberry, Ash, Brambles, Black Cherry, Hawthorn, Wild Garlic, Wild Onion, and Japanese Honeysuckle
Red Maple and Black Gum	Sweet Gum, Ground-cedar, and and Highbush Blueberry	Willow Oak, Shadbush, Winterberry, Oaks, Peat Moss (in depressions), Scrub Pine, and Huckleberry
Red Maple	Black Gum, and Poison Ivy	Sweet Gum, Willow Oak, Haircap Moss, Pin Oak, Greenbriar, Highbush Blueberry, Soft Rush, and Sedge
Red Maple and Sweet Gum	Sweet Pepperbush, Greenbriar, and Black Gum	Swamp Azalea, Inkberry, Rose, Willow Oak, Brambles, Net-veined Chain Fern, Sedge, Sweet Bay, Highbush Blueberry, and American Holly
Loblolly Pine	Sweet Gum, Red Maple, Poison Ivy, and Highbush Blueberry	Inkberry, Sweet Bay, Virginia Creeper, Greenbriar, American Holly, Ironwood, Black Gum and Beech

County. Examples of temporarily flooded forested communities are presented in Tables 15 and 16.

Two types of evergreen forested wetlands are found in Delaware: (1) loblolly pine wetlands, and (2) Atlantic white cedar swamps. The former type is more widespread and may occupy rather large areas, while the latter is relatively uncommon and limited to rather small stands in general. Loblolly pine wetlands occur in both seasonally flooded and temporarily flooded situations, whereas white cedar is usually associated with seasonally flooded areas and freshwater tidal wetlands.

Loblolly pine, although dominant, is often mixed in varying proportions with other trees, including red maple, sweet gum, Atlantic white cedar, sweet bay, and American holly (Plate III.d.). Less common associated trees are water oak (*Quercus nigra*), beech, ironwood, and black gum. The underlying shrub thicket is composed of several species, including highbush blueberry, inkberry, sweet pepperbush, swamp azalea, and wax myrtle. Occasionally elderberry and shadbush (*Amelanchier* spp.) are present. Greenbriars (*Smilax* spp.) and poison ivy may be common, especially at drier sites. Herbaceous plants scattered on the forest floor include skunk cabbage and ferns (e.g., cinnamon, marsh, net-veined chain, and royal) in seasonally flooded areas. Peat moss may be common in wetter depressions, while other mosses also occur.

Historically more abundant, Atlantic white cedar wetlands today are generally confined to rather small stands. Fleming (1978) describes several cedar areas. While white cedar dominates, other trees are intermixed such as sweet bay, loblolly pine, pond pine (*Pinus serotina*), black gum, and green ash. Associated shrubs may include smooth alder, inkberry, highbush blueberry, bayberry, evergreen bayberry (*Myrica heterophylla*), sweet pepperbush, maleberry, deerberry (*Vaccinium stramineum*), swamp rose, and poison ivy. Laurel greenbriar (*Smilax laurifolia*) and redberry greenbriar (*Smilax walteri*) may be present. Emergent groundcover often includes several ferns: royal, marsh, net-veined chain, and Virginia chain (*Woodwardia virginica*). Lizard's-tail may also be present. Fleming (1978) describes a mixed community of pond pine, water oak, and Atlantic white cedar, where Spanish oak (*Quercus falcata*), red maple, American holly, and sweet bay occur as associates.

Lacustrine Wetlands

The Lacustrine System is principally a deepwater habitat system of lakes, reservoirs and deep ponds. Consequently, as in the Riverine System, wetlands are generally limited to shallow waters and exposed shorelines. While algae are probably more abundant in these waters, the vascular macrophytes are more readily

46

observed. A variety of life forms can be recognized, including: (1) free-floating plants, (2) rooted vascular floating-leaved plants, (3) submergent plants, and (4) emergent plants. The first three groups of vascular plants form aquatic beds, while the latter represents nonpersistent emergent wetlands.

Lacustrine Aquatic Beds

Floating-leaved and free-floating aquatic beds are common in lacustrine shallow waters. Dominant floating-leaved species may include spatterdock, white water lily, and water shield. Duckweeds (*Lemna* spp., *Spirodela polyrhiza,* and *Wolffia columbiana*) may comprise the free-floating beds. Bladderworts (*Utricularia* spp.) are also free-floating, but are typically submerged. Submergent aquatic beds are less conspicuous. Lacustrine submergent plants may include pondweeds, bushy pondweeds (*Najas* spp.), wild celery (*Vallisneria americana*), waterweeds (*Elodea* spp.), water milfoils (*Myriophyllum* spp.), mermaidweed, and coontail (*Ceratophyllum demersum*). An introduced pest species, *Hydrilla verticillata*, is a major pond management problem in Sussex County (D. Hardin, pers. comm.).

Nonpersistent Emergent Wetlands

Emergent wetlands frequently form along the shore-lines of lakes and deep ponds (Figure 17). Common nonpersistent plants may include arrowheads, spatter-dock, three-way sedge (*Dulichium arundinaceum*), spikerushes, burreeds, smartweeds, manna grasses, pickerelweeds, and arrow arum. In addition to these species, persistent plants like cattails, water willow, blue flag, alders, swamp rose, rushes, and buttonbush may comprise all or part of lacustrine boundaries. These persistent wetlands, however, fall within the Palustrine System according to Cowardin and others (1979) and are discussed in the preceding section.

Rare and Endangered Wetland Plants

Due to its geographical position, Delaware represents the northern range limit for many southern plants and the southern limit for many northern species. Consequently, numerous rare plants exist in the state and the majority are associated with wetlands. Many rare wetland plants have been listed in the appendix of this report. For more information on these and other rare plants in Delaware, the reader is referred to Tucker and others (1979).

At the national level, 20 of Delaware's plants are under review as being Federally endangered or threatened (likely to become endangered within the foreseeable future) throughout all or a significant part of their range in the United States. Seventeen of them grow in wetlands: Hirst's panic grass (*Panicum hirstii*), Nuttall's

Tiner

Figure 17. Aquatic beds and fringing emergent wetlands are common in many inland lakes and ponds.

micranthemum (*Hemianthus micranthemoides*), Torrey's muhly (*Muhlenbergia torreyana*), Canby's dropwort (*Oxypolis canbyi*), sensitive joint vetch (*Aeschynomene virginica*), sea-beach pigweed (*Amaranthus pumilus*), Pine Barrens boneset (*Eupatorium resinosum*), Darlington's spurge (*Euphorbia purpurea*), swamp pink (*Helonias bullata*), Knieskern's beaked rush (*Rhynchospora knieskernii*), swamp beggar-ticks (*Bidens bidentoides*), Barrett's sedge (*Carex barrattii*), Parker's pipewort (*Eriocaulon parkeri*), Pine Barrens gentian (*Gentiana autumnalis*), Boykin's lobelia (*Lobelia boykinii*), bog asphodel (*Narthecium americanum*), and awned meadow beauty (*Rhexia aristosa*). One of these, Canby's dropwort has been proposed for endangered status and should be listed in early 1986 (R. Dyer, pers. comm.).

Summary

Plant composition of Delaware's wetlands is diverse and complex. Major vegetation differences can be easily seen between the salt and brackish marshes that dominate tidal areas and the forested wetlands that abound in the interior. Yet, even within major vegetative classes of wetlands, significant differences in community structure are apparent. These variations are largely due to several factors including hydrology (water regime), soil type, salinity, human activities (e.g., channelization and other drainage, timber harvest, deposition of fill, and water pollution), and natural events such as fire. Consequently, a wide variety of wetland plant communities exist and they represent an essential part of Delaware's landscape diversity, fish and wildlife habitats, and natural heritage.

References

Bourn, W.S. and C. Cottam. 1950. Some Biological Effects of Ditching Tidewater Marshes. U.S. Fish and Wildlife Service. Res. Rept. 19. 17 pp.

Clarke, R.D. 1978. Ecology of Spartina alterniflora. Master's thesis. University of Delaware, Newark.

Cowardin, L.M., V. Carter, F.C. Golet, and E.T. LaRoe. 1979. Classification of Wetlands and Deepwater Habitats of the United States. U.S. Fish and Wildlife Service. FWS/OBS-79/31. 103 pp.

Daiber, F.C., L.L. Thornton, K.A. Bolster, T.G. Campbell, O.W. Crichton, G.L. Esposito, D.R. Jones, and J.M. Tyrawski. 1976. An Atlas of Delaware's Wetlands and Estuarine Resources. Tech. Rept. No. 2. Delaware Coastal Mgmt. Program, College of Marine Studies, University of Delaware, Newark. 528 pp.

Fleming, L.M. 1978. Delaware's Outstanding Natural Areas and Their Preservation. Delaware Nature Education Society, Hockessin, DE. 422 pp.

Jones, D.R. 1978. Density, distribution, and productivity of small mammals on the Canary Creek marsh, Delaware. Master's thesis. University of Delaware, Newark.

Kennard, W.C., M.W. Lefor, and D.L. Civco. 1983. Analysis of

Coastal Marsh Ecosystems: Effects of Tides on Vegetational Change. Univ. of Connecticut, Institute of Water Resources, Storrs, CT. Res. Proj. Tech. Completion Rept. B-014 CONN. 140 pp.

Martin, W.E. 1959. The vegetation of Island Beach State Park, New Jersey. Ecol. Monogr. 29(1): 1-46.

Nixon, S.W. 1982. The Ecology of New England High Salt Marshes: A Community Profile. U.S. Fish and Wildlife Service. FWS/OBS-81/55. 70 pp.

Odum, W.E., T.J. Smith III, J.K. Hoover, and C.C. McIvor. 1984. The Ecology of Tidal Freshwater Marshes of the United States East Coast: A Community Profile. U.S. Fish and Wildlife Service. FWS/OBS-83/17. 177 pp.

Parker, N.H. 1976. The distribution, growth, and life history of Melampus bidentatus (Gastropoda: Pulmonata) in the Delaware Bay region. Master's thesis. University of Delaware, Newark.

Penfound, W.T. 1952. Southern swamps and marshes. Bot. Rev. 18: 413-446.

Pennock, J.R. 1981. The role of Spartina alterniflora detritus in the nutrition of the American oyster, Crassostrea virginica. Master's thesis. University of Delaware, Newark.

Phillips, N.W. 1978. Spatial distribution and population structure of Orchestia (Amphipoda: Talitridae) in the Canary Creek marsh. Master's thesis. University of Delaware, Newark.

Rennis, D.S. 1978. Movement and size distribution of immature Fundulus heteroclitus (Linnaeus) on a tidal marsh surface. Master's thesis. University of Delaware, Newark.

Roman, C.T. 1981. Detrital exchange processes of a Delaware salt marsh. Ph.D. dissertation. University of Delaware, Newark.

Roman, C.T., and F.C. Daiber. 1984. Aboveground and belowground primary production dynamics of two Delaware Bay tidal marshes. Bull. Torr. Bot. Club III: 34-41.

Silberhorn, G.M. 1982. Common Plants of the Mid-Atlantic Coast. A Field Guide. John Hopkins University Press, Baltimore, MD. 256 pp.

Simek, E.M. 1981. Phytoplankton production in a marsh-dominated estuary. Ph.D. dissertation. University of Delaware, Newark.

Simpson, R.L., R.E. Good, M.A. Leck, and D.F. Whigham. 1983. The ecology of freshwater tidal wetlands. BioScience 33:255-259.

Sipple, W.S. 1977. A tentative description of the vegetation and flora of some unique "pothole" wetlands on the Delmarva Peninsula. Unpublished mimeo. 5 pp.

Teskey, R.O. and T.M. Hinckley. 1977. Impact of Water Level Changes on Woody Riparian and Wetland Communities. Vol. I: Plant and Soil Responses to Flooding. U.S. Fish and Wildlife Service. FWS/OBS-77/58. 30 pp.

Tucker, A.O., N.H. Dill, C.R. Broome, C.E. Phillips, and M.J. Maciarello. 1979. Rare and Endangered Vascular Plant Species in Delaware. U.S. Fish and Wildlife Service, Newton Corner, MA. 89 pp.

Tyrawski, J.M. 1977. Ecology of the common reedgrass (Phragmites communis Trin.) in Delaware wetlands. Master's thesis. University of Delaware, Newark.

U.S.D.A. Soil Conservation Service. 1982. National List of Scientific Plant Names. Vol I. List of Plant Names. SCS-TP-159. 416 pp.

U.S. Fish and Wildlife Service. 1982. Preliminary list of hydrophytes for the northeastern United States. Unpublished mimeo.

Van House, M.P. 1981. A re-examination of the zooplankton community of a Delaware tidal stream. Master's thesis. University of Delaware, Newark.

Watrud, J. 1981. The relationship of meiofaunal ATP to marsh vegetation. Master's thesis. University of Delaware, Newark.

Whitlatch, R.B. 1982. The Ecology of New England Tidal Flats: A Community Profile. U.S. Fish and Wildlife Service. FWS/OBS-81/01. 125 pp.

Winkler, J. 1981. Movement patterns of the meadow vole, Microtus pennsylvanicus, in a Delaware tidal marsh. Master's thesis. University of Delaware, Newark.

CHAPTER 7.

Wetland Values

Introduction

Delaware's wetlands have been traditionally used for hunting, trapping, fishing, timber, and livestock grazing. These uses tend to preserve the wetland integrity, although the qualitative nature of wetlands may be modified, especially by forestry practices. Unfortunately, human uses are not limited to these activities, but also include destructive actions such as drainage for agriculture and silviculture and filling for industrial or residential development. In the past, many people considered wetlands as wastelands whose best use could only be attained through "reclamation projects." To the contrary, wetlands in their natural state provide a wealth of values to society (Table 17). These benefits can be divided into three basic categories: (1) fish and wildlife values, (2) environmental quality values, and (3) socio-economic values. The following discussion emphasizes the more important values of Delaware's wetlands and significant national and regional values. Numerous Delaware wetlands have been identified as outstanding natural areas by Fleming (1978). For an indepth examination of wetland values, the reader is referred to **Wetland Functions and Values: The State of Our Understanding** (Greeson, *et al.* 1979). In addition, the Service has created a wetland values database which contains abstracts of over 2000 articles (Stuber 1983).

Table 17. List of major wetland values.

Fish and Wildlife Values

- Fish and Shellfish Habitat
- Waterfowl and Other Bird Habitat
- Furbearer and Other Wildlife Habitat

Environmental Quality Values

- Water Quality Maintenance
  - Pollution Filter
  - Sediment Removal
  - Oxygen Production
  - Nutrient Recycling
  - Chemical and Nutrient
  - Absorption
- Aquatic Productivity
- Microclimate Regulator
- World Climate (Ozone layer)

Socio-Economic Values

- Flood Control
- Wave Damage Protection
- Erosion Control
- Ground-water Recharge
- Water Supply
- Timber and Other Natural Products
- Energy Source (Peat)
- Livestock Grazing
- Fish and Shellfishing
- Hunting and Trapping
- Recreation
- Aesthetics
- Education and Scientific Research

Fish and Wildlife Values

Fish and wildlife utilize wetlands in a variety of ways. Some animals are totally wetland-dependent, spending their entire lives in wetlands. Others use wetlands only for specific reasons, such as reproduction and nursery grounds, feeding, and resting areas during migration. Many upland animals visit wetlands to obtain drinking water. Wetlands are also essential for survival of numerous endangered animals. Daiber (1982) describes in detail the interrelationships between animals and coastal marshes.

Fish and Shellfish Habitat

Both inland and coastal wetlands are essential to maintaining important fish populations. Estuarine wetlands are important producers of shrimp, crabs, oysters and clams for human consumption.

Approximately two-thirds of the major U.S. commercial fishes depend on estuaries and salt marshes for nursery or spawning grounds (McHugh 1966). Among the more familiar wetland-dependent fishes are menhaden, bluefish, fluke, sea trout, mullet, croaker, striped bass, and drum. Coastal marshes along the Atlantic and Gulf Coasts are most important in this regard. Between Manasquan and Cape May, New Jersey, Wang and Kernehan (1979) found 40 estuarine spawning fishes and 136 species using estuaries as nursery grounds. According to state fisheries biologists, about 98% of Delaware's commercially-important fishes are wetland-dependent. Common fishes in Delaware's tidal marshes and estuaries include the American eel, alewife, American shad, blueback herring, carp, white catfish, channel catfish, brown bullhead, white perch, striped bass, yellow perch, silver perch, sea trout, Atlantic croaker, summer flounder and winter flounder (Martin 1974). Menhaden and spot are also abundant in tidal creeks.

Coastal wetlands are also essential for important shellfish like bay scallops, blue crabs, oysters and clams. Estuarine aquatic beds, in general, also provide important cover for juvenile fishes and other estuarine organisms (Good, *et al.* 1978).

Figure 18. Migratory birds depend on wetlands: (a) black duck, (b) osprey, (c) common egret, and (d) yellow warbler.

Freshwater fishes also find wetlands essential for survival. In fact, nearly all freshwater fishes can be considered wetland-dependent because: (1) many species feed in wetlands or upon wetland-produced food, (2) many fishes use wetlands as nursery grounds and (3) almost all important recreational fishes spawn in the aquatic portions of wetlands (Peters, *et al.* 1979). Important freshwater fishes in Delaware include large-mouth bass, white and black crappies, yellow perch, bluegill, pumpkinseed, brown bullhead and chain pickerel. Anadromous fishes, i.e., alewife, American shad, and blueback herring, spend their adult lives in Delaware Bay and the Atlantic Ocean and return to freshwater rivers to spawn, while the blueback herring may also spawn in brackish waters (Daiber, *et al.* 1976). All of these species utilize tidal marshes and estuaries as nursery grounds.

Waterfowl and Other Bird Habitat

In addition to providing year-round habitats for resident birds, wetlands are especially important as breeding grounds, overwintering areas and feeding grounds for migratory waterfowl and numerous other birds (Figure 18). Both coastal and inland wetlands serve these valuable functions.

Salt marshes along the Atlantic Coast are used for nesting by birds such as black ducks, laughing gulls, Forster's terns, clapper rails, blue-winged teals, willets, marsh hawks, sharp-tailed sparrows, and seaside sparrows. During the NWI survey, black ducks were observed nesting in the high-tide bush zone. Wading birds like great blue herons, black-crowned night herons, little blue herons, glossy ibises, common egrets and snowy egrets also feed in Delaware's coastal wetlands and nest in adjacent woody vegetation (Daiber, *et al.* 1976). The U.S. Fish and Wildlife Service (Erwin and Korschgen 1979) has identified nesting colonies of coastal water birds in Delaware and other northeastern states. Atlantic coastal marshes are important feeding and stopover areas for migrating snow geese, peregrine falcons, shorebirds and wading birds. Intertidal mudflats are principal feeding grounds for migratory shorebirds (e.g., oystercatchers, ringed plovers and knots), while swallows can often be seen feeding on flying insects over the adjacent marshes.

Delaware's salt marshes are also important wintering grounds for black ducks, brant, Canada geese, greater snow geese, and mallards in the Atlantic Flyway.

Forty-eight species of birds were reported nesting in neighboring New Jersey's freshwater tidal marshes (Hawkins and Leck 1977). They include redwinged blackbirds, long-billed marsh wrens, least bitterns, clapper rails, American goldfinches, swamp sparrows, Indigo buntings, common yellowthroats, yellow warblers, Traill's flycatchers, wood ducks, green herons, and common gallinules. Many of these birds utilize nontidal wetlands as well for nesting. McCormick (1970) found 119 species of birds at Tinicum Marsh, outside of Philadelphia.

Delaware's inland wetlands serve as important nesting, feeding and resting areas for other resident and migrating birds. Common breeding waterfowl include black duck, mallard, blue-winged teal, wood duck and gadwall. Black ducks also use swamp creeks in winter, often during severe coastal storms. In neighboring New Jersey, from 40-45 nesting bird species were observed in hardwood swamps (Wander 1980). Great-crested flycatchers, pine warblers, towhees, chickadees, titmouses, prothonotary warblers, scarlet tanagers, vireos, acadian flycatchers, ovenbirds, black and white warblers, catbirds, yellowthroats, brown creepers, hooded warblers and black-throated green warblers were among the most important breeding birds. This study suggested that swamp size was somewhat less important than vegetative composition in determining avian diversity. American bitterns, long-billed marsh wrens, redwinged blackbirds, swamp sparrows and song sparrows nest in freshwater marshes, while veeries and yellowthroats utilize forested wetlands and wet thickets, respectively.

Wetlands are, therefore, crucial for the existence of many birds, ranging from waterfowl and shorebirds to songbirds. Some spend their entire lives in wetland environments, while others primarily use wetlands for breeding, feeding or resting.

Furbearer and Other Wildlife Habitat

If a Delaware fur trapper is asked about the value of wetlands, he is likely to reply that they produce furbearers like muskrats (Figure 19). Muskrats inhabit both coastal and inland marshes in Delaware, but are most abundant in slightly brackish marshes (B. Moyer, pers. comm.). Other wetland-utilizing furbearers include beaver, otter, mink, raccoons, skunks and weasels. Smaller mammals also frequent wetlands such as marsh and swamp rabbits, numerous mice and shrews, while larger mammals like deer may also be observed. Deer often use forested wetlands and treed hummocks within tidal marshes for escape cover, according to state wildlife biologists.

Besides the animals previously mentioned, other forms of wildlife make their homes in wetlands. Turtles, reptiles, and amphibians are important residents. Turtles are most common in freshwater marshes and ponds. The more important ones nationally are the painted, spotted, Blanding's, map, pond, musk and snapping turtles (Clark 1979). Along the coast, the diamond-backed terrapin is a common denizen of salt marshes.

Many snakes also inhabit wetlands with water snakes being most abundant throughout the U.S. (Clark 1979). Garter snakes are also common in Delaware's inland wetlands.

Nearly all of the approximately 190 species of amphibians in North America are wetland-dependent, at least for breeding (Clark 1979). Frogs occur in many freshwater wetlands and common frogs include the bull, green, leopard, mink, pickerel, wood and chorus frogs and spring peepers. Many salamanders use temporary ponds or wetlands for breeding, although they may spend most of the year in uplands. Numbers of amphibians, even in small wetlands can be astonishing. For example, 1,600 salamanders and 3,800 frogs and toads were found in a small gum pond (less than 100 feet wide) in Georgia (Wharton 1978).

Environmental Quality Values

Besides providing homes for fish and wildlife, wetlands play a less conspicuous but nonetheless important role in maintaining high environmental

FWS

Figure 19. The muskrat inhabits both coastal and inland emergent wetlands in Delaware.

quality, especially for aquatic habitats. They do this in a number of ways, including purifying natural waters by removing nutrients, chemical and organic pollutants, and sediment and producing food which supports aquatic life.

Water Quality Improvement

Wetlands help maintain good water quality or improve degraded waters in several ways: (1) nutrient removal and retention, (2) processing chemical and organic wastes, and (3) reducing sediment load of water. Wetlands are particularly good water filters because of their location between land and water. Thus, they can both intercept runoff from land before it reaches the water and help filter nutrients, wastes and sediment from flooding waters. Clean waters are important to people as well as to fish and wildlife.

First, wetlands remove nutrients, especially nitrogen and phosphorus, from flooding waters for plant growth and help prevent eutrophication or over-enrichment of natural waters. Freshwater tidal wetlands are important in reducing nutrient and heavy metal loading from urban runoff in the upper Delaware River estuary (Simpson, et al. 1983b). It is, however, possible to overload a wetland and thereby reduce its ability to perform this function. Every wetland has a limited capacity to absorb nutrients and individual wetlands differ in their ability to do so.

Wetlands have been shown to be excellent removers of waste products from water. Sloey and others (1978) summarize the value of freshwater wetlands at removing nitrogen and phosphorus from the water and address management issues. They note that certain wetland plants are so efficient at this task that some artificial waste treatment systems use these plants. For example, the Max Planck Institute of Germany has a patent to create such systems, where a bulrush (*Scirpus lacustris*) is the primary waste removal agent. Numerous scientists have proposed that certain types of wetlands be used to process domestic wastes and some wetlands are already used for this purpose (Sloey, et al. 1978; Carter, et al. 1979; Kadlec 1979). Wetlands may be valuable as tertiary treatment systems. It must be kept in mind that individual wetlands have a finite capacity for natural assimilation of excess nutrients and research is needed to determine this threshold.

Perhaps the best example of the importance of wetlands for water quality improvement is Tinicum Marsh (Grant and Patrick 1970). Tinicum Marsh is a 512-acre freshwater tidal marsh lying just south of Philadelphia, Pennsylvania. Three sewage treatment plants discharge treated sewage into marsh waters. On a daily basis, it was shown that this marsh removes from flooding waters: 7.7 tons of biological oxygen demand, 4.9 tons of phosphorus, 4.3 tons of ammonia, and 138 pounds of nitrate. In addition, Tinicum Marsh adds 20 tons of oxygen to the water each day.

Swamps also have the capacity for removing water pollutants. Bottomland forested wetlands along the Alcovy River in Georgia filter impurities from flooding waters. Human and chicken wastes grossly pollute the river upstream, but after passing through less than 3 miles of swamp, the river's water quality is significantly improved. The value of the 2,300-acre Alcovy River Swamp for water pollution control was estimated at $1 million per year (Wharton 1970). Many of Delaware's forested wetlands may assimilate excess nutrients from adjacent agricultural land and other upland development.

Wetlands also play a valuable role in reducing turbidity of flooding waters. This is especially important for aquatic life and for reducing siltation of ports, harbors, rivers and reservoirs. Removal of sediment load is also valuable because sediments often transport absorbed nutrients, pesticides, heavy metals and other toxins which pollute our Nation's waters (Boto and Patrick 1979). Depressional wetlands should retain all of the sediment entering them (Novitski 1978). In Wisconsin, watersheds with 40% coverage by lakes and wetlands had 90% less sediment in water than watersheds with no lakes or wetlands (Hindall 1975). Creekbanks of salt marshes typically support more productive vegetation than the marsh interior. Deposition of silt is accentuated at the water-marsh interface, where vegetation slows the velocity of water causing sediment to drop out of solution. In addition to improving water quality, this process adds nutrients to the creekside marsh which leads to higher plant productivity (DeLaune, et al. 1978).

The U.S. Army Corps of Engineers has investigated the use of marsh vegetation to lower turbidity of dredged disposal runoff and to remove contaminants. In a 50-acre impoundment near Georgetown, South Carolina, after passing through about 2,000 feet of marsh vegetation, the effluent turbidity was similar to that of the adjacent river (Lee, et al. 1976). Wetlands have also been proven to be good filters of nutrients and heavy metal loads in dredged disposal effluents (Windom 1977).

Recently, the ability of wetlands to retain heavy metals has been reported (Banus, et al. 1974; Mudroch and Capobianca 1978; Simpson, *et al.* 1983c). Wetland soils have been regarded as primary sinks for heavy metals, while wetland plants may play a more limited role. Waters flowing through urban areas often have heavy concentrations of heavy metals (e.g., cadmium, chromium, copper, nickel, lead, and zinc). The ability of freshwater tidal wetlands along the Delaware River in New Jersey to sequester and hold heavy metals has been documented (Good, *et al.* 1975; Whigham and Simpson 1976; Simpson, *et al.* 1983a, 1983b, 1983c). Additional study is needed to better understand retention mechanisms and capacities in these and other types of wetlands.

Aquatic Productivity

Wetlands are among the most productive ecosystems in the world and some types may be the highest, rivaling our best cornfields (Figure 20). Wetlands plants are particularly efficient converters of solar energy. Through photosynthesis, plants convert sunlight into plant material or biomass and produce oxygen as a by-product. Other materials, such as organic matter, nutrients, heavy metals, and sediment, are also captured by wetlands and either stored in the sediment or converted to biomass (Simpson, *et al.* 1983a). This biomass serves as food for a multitude of animals, both aquatic and terrestrial. For example, many waterfowl depend heavily on seeds of marsh plants, especially during the winter, while muskrat eat cattail and bulrush tubers and young shoots. Roman and Daiber (1984) have studied above and below ground primary productivity of several plants in two Delaware tidal marshes.

Although direct grazing of wetland plants is generally limited, their major food value is reached upon death when plants fragment to form "detritus." This detritus forms the base of an aquatic food web which supports higher consumers, e.g., commercial fishes. This relationship is especially well-documented for coastal areas. Animals, like zooplankton, shrimp, snails, crabs, clams, worms, killifish and mullet, eat "detritus" or graze upon the bacteria, fungi, diatoms and protozoa growing on its surfaces (Crow and Macdonald 1979; de la Cruz 1979). Forage fishes (e.g., anchovies, sticklebacks,

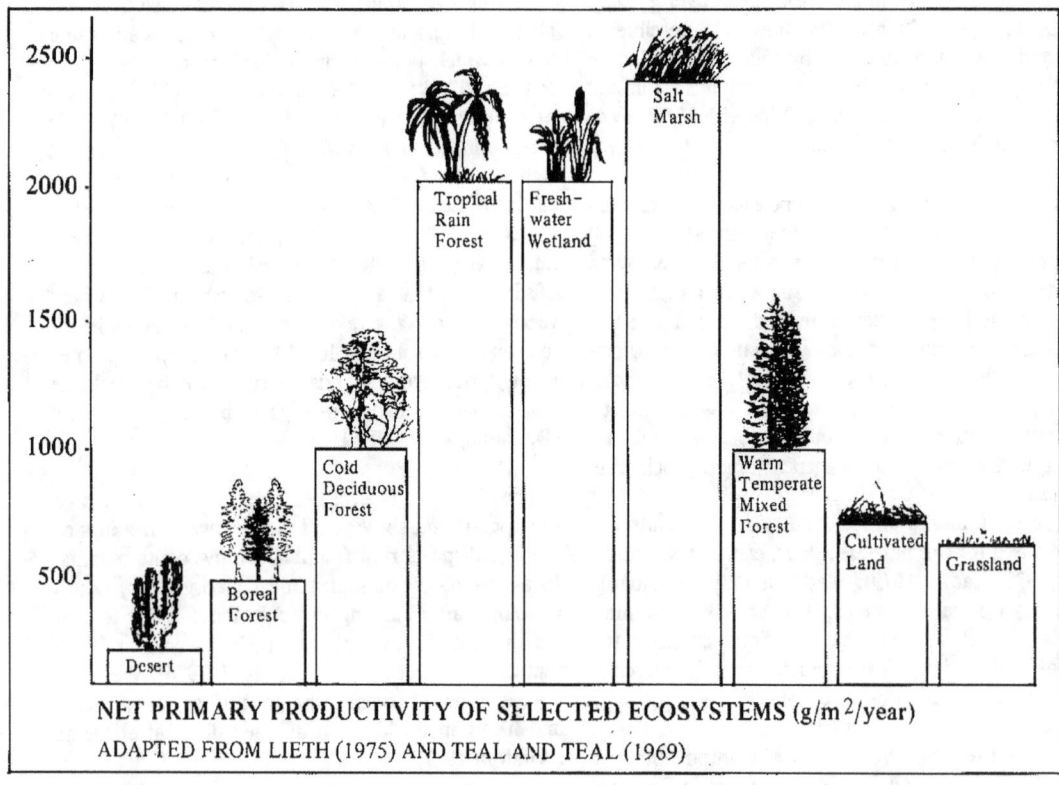

NET PRIMARY PRODUCTIVITY OF SELECTED ECOSYSTEMS (g/m^2/year)

ADAPTED FROM LIETH (1975) AND TEAL AND TEAL (1969)

Figure 20. Relative productivity of wetland ecosystems in relation to other ecosystems (redrawn from Newton 1981). Salt marshes and freshwater wetlands are among the most productive ecosystems.

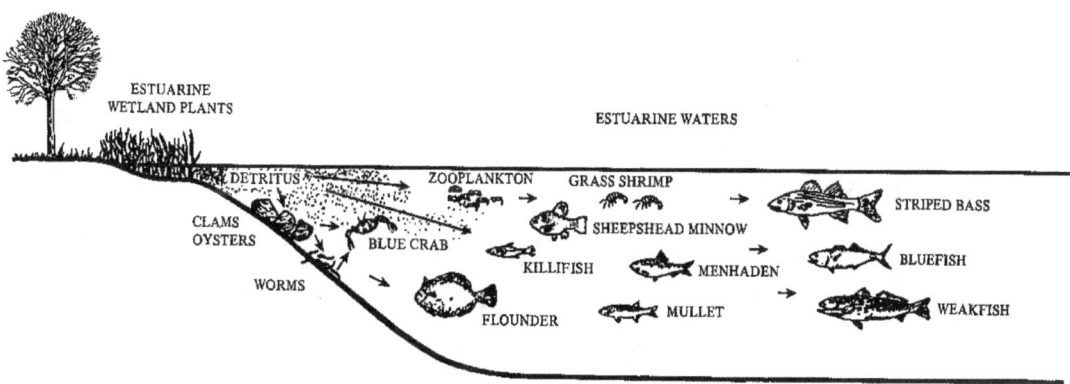

Figure 21. Simplified food pathways from estuarine wetland vegetation to commercial and recreational fishes of importance to people.

killifishes, and silversides) and grass shrimp are the primary food for commercial and recreational fishes, including bluefish, flounder, weakfish, and white perch (Sugihara, *et al.* 1979). A simplified food web for Delaware estuaries is presented as Figure 21. Thus, wetlands can be regarded as the farmlands of the aquatic environment where great volumes of food are produced annually. The majority of non-marine aquatic animals also depend, either directly or indirectly, on this food source.

Socio-economic Values

The more tangible benefits of wetlands to mankind may be considered socio-economic values and they include flood and storm damage protection, erosion control, water supply and ground-water recharge, harvest of natural products, livestock grazing and recreation. Since these values provide either dollar savings or financial profit, they are more easily understood and appreciated by most people.

Flood and Storm Damage Protection

In their natural condition, wetlands serve to temporarily store flood waters, thereby protecting downstream property owners from flood damage. After all, such flooding has been the driving force in creating these wetlands to begin with. This flood storage function also helps to slow the velocity of water and lower wave heights, which reduces the water's erosive potential. Rather than having all flood waters flowing rapidly downstream and destroying private property and crops, wetlands slow the flow of water, store it for a period of time and slowly release stored waters downstream

(Figure 22). This becomes increasingly important in urban areas, where development has increased the rate and volume of surface water runoff and the potential for flood damage.

In 1975, 107 people were killed by flood waters in the U.S. and potential property damage for the year was estimated to be $3.4 billion (U.S. Water Resources Council 1978). Almost half of all flood damage was suffered by farmers as crops and livestock were destroyed and productive land was covered by water or lost to erosion. Approximately 134 million acres of the conterminous U.S. have severe flooding problems. Of this, 2.8 million acres are urban land and 92.8 million acres are agricultural land (U.S. Water Resources Council 1977). Many of these flooded farmlands are wetlands or previously drained wetlands. Although regulations and ordinances required by the Federal Insurance Administration reduce flood losses from urban land, agricultural losses are expected to remain at present levels or increase as more wetland is put into crop production. Protection of wetlands is, therefore, an important means to minimizing flood damages in the future.

The U.S. Army Corps of Engineers has recognized the value of wetlands for flood storage in Massachusetts. In the early 1970's, they considered various alternatives to providing flood protection in the lower Charles River watershed near Boston, including: (1) a 55,000 acre-foot reservoir, (2) extensive walls and dikes, and (3) perpetual protection of 8,500 acres of wetland (U.S. Army Corps of Engineers 1976). If 40% of the Charles River wetlands were destroyed, flood damages would increase by at least $3 million annually. Loss of all basin wetlands would cause an average annual flood damage cost of $17 million (Thibodeau

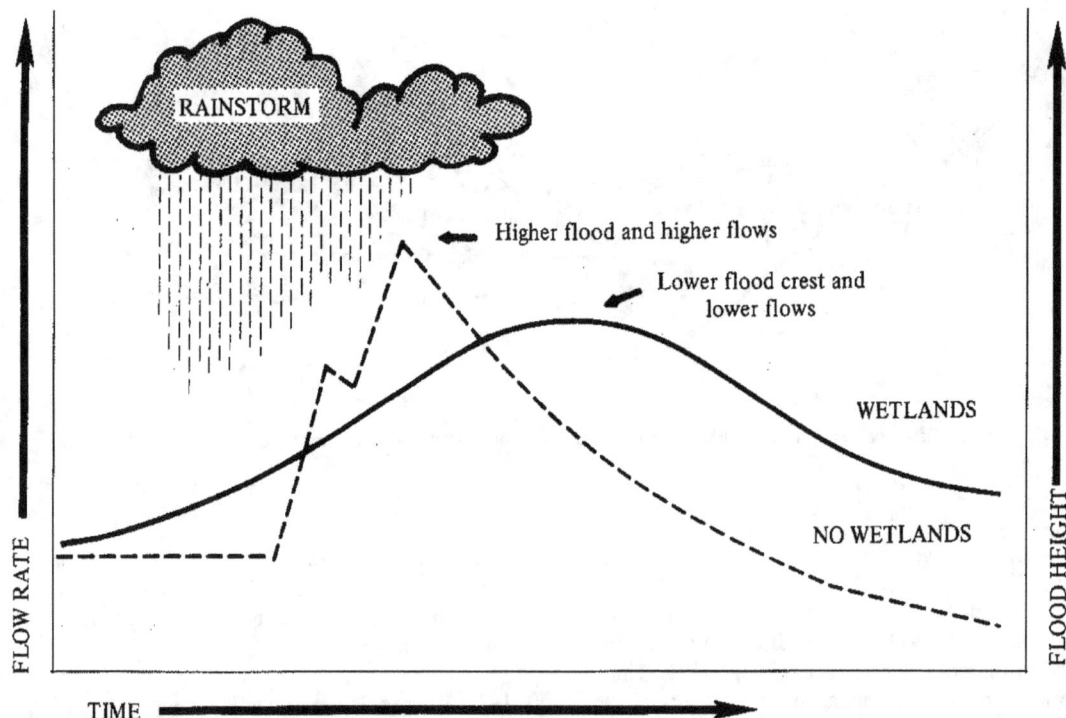

Figure 22. Wetland values in reducing flood crests and flow rates after rainstorms (adapted from Kusler 1983).

and Ostro 1981). The Corps concluded that wetlands protection - "Natural Valley Storage" - was the least-cost solution to flooding problems. In 1983, they completed acquisition of approximately 8,500 acres of Charles River wetlands for flood protection.

This protective value of wetlands has also been reported for other areas. Undeveloped floodplain wetlands in New Jersey protect against flood damages (Robichaud and Buell 1973). In eastern Pennsylvania, the 1955 floods washed out all but two bridges along one stream; these remaining bridges lay immediately downstream of the Cranberry Bog (Goodwin and Niering 1975). A Wisconsin study projected that floods may be lowered as much as 80% in watersheds with many wetlands compared with similar basins with little or no wetlands (Novitski 1978). Pothole wetlands in the Devils Lake Basin of North Dakota store nearly 75% of the total runoff (Ludden, *et al.* 1983). Many of Delaware's wetlands undoubtedly are important for storing runoff and reducing flood damages.

Recent studies at National Wildlife Refuges in North Dakota and Minnesota have demonstrated the role of wetlands in reducing streamflow. Inflow into the Agassiz National Wildlife Refuge and the Thief River Wildlife Management Area was 5,000 cubic feet per second (cfs), while outflow as only 1,400 cfs. Storage capacity of those areas reduced flood peaks at Crookston, Minnesota by 1.5 feet and at Grand Forks, North Dakota by 0.5 feet (Bernot 1979). Drainage of wetlands was the most important land-use practice causing flood problems in a North Dakota watershed (Malcolm 1978; Malcolm 1979). Even northern peat bogs reduce peak rates of streamflow from snow melt and heavy summer rains (Verry and Boelter 1979). Destruction of wetlands through floodplain development and wetland drainage have been partly responsible for recent major flood disasters throughout the country.

Besides reducing flood levels and potential damage, wetlands may buffer the land from storm wave damage. Salt marshes are considered important shoreline stabilizers due to their wave dampening effect. A fringe of salt marsh grasses as narrow as eight feet can reduce wave energy by over 50% (Knudson, *et al.* 1982). Forested wetlands along lakes and large rivers may function similarly.

Erosion Control

Located between watercourses and uplands, wetlands help protect uplands from erosion. Wetland vegetation can reduce shoreline erosion in several ways, including:

(1) increasing durability of the sediment through binding with its roots, (2) dampening waves through friction and (3) reducing current velocity through friction (Dean 1979). This process also helps reduce turbidity and thereby improves water quality.

Obviously, trees are good stabilizers of river banks. Their roots bind the soil, making it more resistant to erosion, while their trunks and branches slow the flow of flooding waters and dampen wave heights. The banks of some rivers have not been eroded for 100 to 200 years due to the presence of trees (Leopold and Wolman 1957; Wolman and Leopold 1957; Sigafoos 1964). Among the grass and grass-like plants, bulrushes and reed have been regarded as the best at withstanding wave and current action (Kadlec and Wentz 1974; Seibert 1968). While most wetland plants need calm or sheltered water for establishment, they will effectively control erosion once established (Kadlec and Wentz 1974; Garbisch 1977).

Wetland vegetation has been successfully planted to reduce erosion along U.S. waters. Willows, alders, ashes, cottonwoods, poplars, maples and elms are particularly good stabilizers (Allen 1979). Successful emergent plants include reed canary grass, reed, cattail, and bulrushes in freshwater areas (Hoffman 1977). Along the Atlantic coast, smooth cordgrass has been quite effective (Woodhouse, *et al.* 1976).

Water Supply and Ground-water Recharge

Most wetlands are areas of ground-water discharge and some may provide sufficient quantities of water for public use. In Massachusetts, 40-50% of freshwater wetlands may be valuable potential sources of drinking water, since at least 60 municipalities have public wells in or very near wetlands (Motts and Heeley 1973). Prairie pothole wetlands store water which is important for wildlife and may be used for irrigation and livestock watering by farmers during droughts (Leitch 1981). These situations may hold true for many other states and wetland protection could be instrumental in solving current and future water supply problems.

There is considerable debate over the role of wetlands in ground-water recharge. Recharge potential of wetlands varies according to numerous factors, including wetland type, geographic location, season, soil type, water table action and precipitation. Shrub wetlands in the Pine Barrens of New Jersey may contribute to ground-water recharge (Ballard 1979). Depressional wetlands like cypress domes in Florida and prairie potholes in the Dakotas may also contribute to ground-

water recharge (Odum, *et al.* 1975; Stewart and Kantrud 1972). Floodplain wetlands also may do this through overbank water storage (Mundorff 1950; Klopatek 1978). These studies and others suggest that additional research is needed to better assess the role of wetlands in ground-water recharge.

Harvest of Natural Products

A variety of natural products are produced by wetlands, including timber, fish and shellfish, wildlife, peat, cranberries, blueberries, and wild rice. Wetland grasses are hayed in many places for winter livestock feed. During other seasons, livestock graze directly in wetlands across the country. Along Delaware Bay, many tidal marshes in New Jersey have been impounded for producing salt hay. These and other products are harvested by man for his use and provide a livelihood for many people.

In the 49 continental states, an estimated 82 million acres of commercial forested wetlands exist (Johnson 1979). These forests provide timber for such uses as homes, furniture, newspapers and firewood. Most of these forests lie east of the Rockies, where trees like oak, gum, cypress, elm, ash and cottonwood are most important. The standing value of southern wetland forests is $8 billion. These southern forests have been harvested for over 200 years without noticeable degradation, thus they can be expected to produce timber for may years to come, unless converted to other uses. Although most of Delaware's forested wetlands are considered inaccessible for commercial harvest, approximately 1,000-2,000 acres may be harvested each year (D. Hardin, pers. comm.). This timber is used for pallets, railroad ties, utility lumber or firewood. The value of an acre of forested wetland for timber ranges from $200-300.

Wetlands also produce fish and wildlife for human use. Commercial fishermen and trappers make a living from these resources. From 1956 to 1975, about 60% of the U.S. commercial landings were fishes and shellfishes that depend on wetlands (Peters, *et al.* 1979). Major commercial species associated with wetlands are menhaden, salmon, shrimp, blue crab and alewife from coastal waters and catfish, carp and buffalo from inland areas. About 98% of Delaware's commercial fisheries consist of estuarine-dependent species. The 1981 harvest amounted to roughly $2 million, with nearly half of this value attributed to blue crabs and oysters (U.S. Department of Commerce 1982). Nationally, furs from beaver, muskrat, mink, nutria, and otter yielded roughly $35.5 million in 1976 (Demms and Pursley 1978). Louisiana is the largest fur-producing state and nearly all furs come from wetland animals. In Delaware, nearly 150,000 muskrats are harvested annually for an estimated value of over $0.5 million, according to state wildlife biologists.

Recreation and Aesthetics

Many recreational activities take place in and around wetlands. Hunting and fishing are popular sports. Waterfowl hunting is a major activity in wetlands, but big game hunting is also important locally. In 1980, 5.3 million people spent $638 million on hunting waterfowl and other migratory birds (U.S. Department of Interior and Department of Commerce 1982). For Delaware, 20,900 people spent over $2 million hunting waterfowl. Saltwater recreational fishing has increased dramatically over the past 20 years, with half of this catch represented by wetland-associated species. In Delaware, virtually all important recreational saltwater fishes are estuarine-dependent. Approximately 210,000 people annually fish for summer flounder, weakfish, striped bass, bluefish, white perch, and Atlantic croaker (D. Hardin, pers. comm.). Moreover, nearly all freshwater fishing is dependent on wetlands. About 35,000 people fish annually in Delaware's inland waters for largemouth bass, black crappie, yellow perch, bluegill, and other fishes (D. Hardin, pers. comm.). In 1975 alone, sportfishermen spent $13.1 billion to catch wetland-dependent fishes in the U.S. (Peters, et al. 1979). Nearly 250,000 people fished in Delaware's waters in 1980, with over 85% participating in saltwater fishing. Recreational fishing in Delaware generates nearly $20 million annually (U.S. Department of Interior and Department of Commerce 1982).

Other recreation in wetlands is largely non-consumptive and involves activities like hiking, nature observation and photography, canoeing and other boating. Many people simply enjoy the beauty and sounds of nature and spend their leisure time walking or boating in or near wetlands observing plant and animal life. This aesthetic value is extremely difficult to evaluate or place a dollar value upon. Nonetheless, it is a very important one because in 1980 alone, 28.8 million people (17% of the U.S. population) took special trips to observe, photograph or feed wildlife. Moreover, about 47% of all Americans showed an active interest in wildlife around their homes (U.S. Department of Interior and Department of Commerce 1982). Between October 1982 and October 1983, Bombay Hook National Wildlife Refuge was visited more than 32,000 times by people mainly interested in observing wildlife. Delaware's wetlands provide residents and visitors with opportunities to view and appreciate a wealth of plants and animals.

Summary

Marshes, swamps and other wetlands are assets to society in their natural state. They provide numerous products for human use and consumption, protect private property and provide recreational and aesthetic appreciation opportunities. Wetlands may also have other values yet unknown to man. For example, a micro-organism from Pine Barrens swamps in New Jersey has been recently discovered to have great value to the drug industry. From this micro-organism, scientists at the Squibb Institute have developed a new family of antibiotics that will be used to cure diseases that are not affected by present antibiotics (Moore 1981). This represents a significant medical breakthrough. If these wetlands were destroyed or grossly polluted, this discovery may not have been possible.

Destruction or alteration of wetlands eliminates or minimizes their values. Drainage of wetlands, for example, eliminates all of the beneficial effects of the marsh on water quality and directly contributes to flooding problems (Lee, et al. 1975). While the wetland landowner can derive financial profit from some of the values mentioned, the general public receives the vast majority of wetland benefits through flood and storm damage control, erosion control, water quality improvement, fish and wildlife resources, and aesthetics. It is, therefore, in the public's best interest to protect wetlands to preserve these values for themselves and for future generations.

References

Allen, H.H. 1979. Role of wetland plants in erosion control of riparian shorelines. In: P.E. Greeson, et al. Wetland Functions and Values: The State of Our Understanding. Amer. Water Resources Association. pp. 403-414.

Ballard, J.T. 1979. Fluxes of water and energy through the Pine Barrens ecosystems. In: R.T.T. Forman (editor). Pine Barrens: Ecosystem and Landscape. Academic Press, Inc., New York, NY. pp. 133-146.

Banus, M., I. Valiela, and J.M. Teal. 1974. Export of lead from salt marshes. Mar. Poll. Bull. 5: 6-9.

Bernot, C. 1979. Water Bank: Keeping Wetlands Wet. The Minnesota Volunteer 42(246): 4.

Boto, K.G. and W.H. Patrick, Jr. 1979. Role of wetlands in the removal of suspended sediments. In: P.E. Greeson, et al. Wetland Functions and Values: The State of Our Understanding. Amer. Water Resources Association. pp. 479-489.

Carter, V., M.S. Bedinger, R.P. Novitski, and W.O. Wilen. 1979. Water resources and wetlands. *In*: P.E. Greeson, *et al.* Wetland Functions and Values: The State of Our Understanding. Amer. Water Resources Association. pp. 344-376.

Clark, J.E. 1979. Fresh water wetlands: habitats for aquatic invertebrates, amphibians, reptiles, and fish. *In*: P.E. Greeson, *et al.* Wetland Functions and Values: The State of Our Understanding. Amer. Resources Assoication. pp. 330-343.

Crow, J.H. and K.B. MacDonald. 1979. Wetland values: secondary production. *In*: P.E. Greeson, *et al.* Wetland Functions and Values: The State of Our Understanding. Amer. Water Resources Association. pp. 146-161.

Daiber, F.C. 1982. Animals of the Tidal Marsh. Van Nostrand Reinhold Company, New York, NY. 422 pp.

Daiber, F.C., L.R. Thornton, K.A. Bolster, T.G. Campbell, O.W. Crichton, G.L. Esposito, D.R. Jones, and J.M. Tyrawski. 1976. An Atlas of Delaware's Wetlands and Estuarine Resources. University of Delaware, College of Marine Studies, Newark. Delaware Coastal Management Program Technical Report. No. 2. 528 pp.

Dean, R.G. 1979. Effects of vegetation on shoreline erosional processes. *In*: P.E. Greeson, *et al.* Wetland Functions and Values: The State of Our Understanding. Amer. Water Resources Association. pp. 415-426.

De La Cruz, A.A. 1979. Production and transport of detritus in wetlands. *In*: P.E. Greeson, *et al.* Wetland Functions and Values: The State of Our Understanding. Amer. Water Resources Association. pp. 162-174.

DeLaune, R.D., W.H. Patrick, Jr., and R.J. Buresk. 1978. Sedimentation rates determined by 137Cs dating in a rapidly accreting salt marsh. Nature 275: 532-533.

Demms, E.F., Jr. and D. Pursley (editors). 1978. North American Furbearers: Their Management, Research and Harvest Status in 1976. International Association of Fish and Wildlife Agencies. 157 pp.

Erwin, R.M. and C.E. Korschgen. 1979. Coastal Waterbird Colonies: Maine to Virginia, 1977. U.S. Fish and Wildlife Service. FWS/OBS-79/08. 647 pp. and appendices.

Fleming, L.M. 1978. Delaware's Outstanding Natural Areas and Their Preservation. Delaware Nature Education Society, Hockessin. 422 pp.

Garbisch, E.W., Jr. 1977. Marsh development for soil erosion. *In*: Proc. of the Workshop on the Role of Vegetation in Stabilization of the Great Lakes Shoreline. Great Lakes Basin Commission, Ann Arbor, MI. pp. 77-94.

Good, R.E., J. Limb, E. Lyszczek, M. Miernik, C. Ogrosky, N. Psuty, J. Ryan, and F. Stickels. 1978. Analysis and Delineation of Submerged Vegetation of Coastal New Jersey: A Case Study of Little Egg Harbor. Rutgers University, Center for Coastal and Environmental Studies, New Brunswick, NJ. 58 pp.

Goodwin, R.H. and W.A. Niering. 1975. Inland Wetlands of the United States. Evaluated as Potential Registered Natural Landmarks. National Park Service, Nat. Hist. Theme Studies, No. 2. 550 pp.

Grant, R.R., Jr. and R. Patrick. 1970. Tinicum Marsh as a water purifier. *In*: Two Studies of Tinicum Marsh. The Conservation Foundation, Washington, DC. pp. 105-123.

Greeson, P.B., J.R. Clark, and J.E. Clark (editors). 1979. Wetland Functions and Values: The State of Our Understanding. Proc. of the National Symposium on Wetlands. November 7-10, 1978. Amer. Water Resources Association, Minneapolis, MN. 674 pp.

Hawkins, P. and C.F. Leck. 1977. Breeding bird communities in a tidal freshwater marsh. Bull. N.J. Acad. Sci. 22(1): 12-17.

Hindall, S.M. 1975. Measurements and Prediction of Sediment Yields in Wisconsin Streams. U.S. Geological Survey Water Resources Investigations 54-75. 27 pp.

Hoffman, G.R. 1977. Artificial establishment of vegetation and effects of fertilizer along shorelines of Lake Oahe and Sakakawea mainstem Missouri River reservoirs. *In*: Proc. of the Workshop on the Role of Vegetation in Stabilization of the Great Lakes Shoreline. Great Lakes Basin Commission, Ann Arbor, MI. pp. 95-109.

Johnson, R.L. 1979. Timber harvests from wetlands. *In*: P.E. Greeson, *et al.* Wetland Functions and Values: The State of Our Understanding. Amer. Water Resources Association. pp. 598-605.

Kadlec, J.A. and W.A. Wentz. 1974. State-of-the-art Survey and Evaluation of Marsh Plant Establishment Techniques: Induced and Natural. Vol. I: Report of Research. Tech. Rept. D-74-9. U.S. Army Engineers Waterways Expt. Station, Vicksburg, MS.

Kadlec, R.H. 1979. Wetlands for tertiary treatment. *In*: P.E. Greeson, *et al.* (editors). Wetland Functions and Values: The State of Our Understanding. Amer. Water Resources Association. pp. 490-504.

Klopatek, J.M. 1978. Nutrient dynamics of freshwater riverine marshes and the role of emergent macrophytes. *In*: R.E. Good, D.F. Whigham, and R.L. Simpson (editors). 1978. Freshwater Wetlands, Ecological Processes and Management Potential. Academic Press, New York, NY. pp. 195-216.

Knudson, P.L., R.A. Brocchu, W.N. Seelig, and M. Inskeep. 1982. Wave dampening in *Spartina alterniflora* marshes. Wetlands (Journal of the Society of Wetland Scientists) 2: 87-104.

Kusler, J.A. 1983. Our National Wetland Heritage. A Protection Guidebook. Environmental Law Institute, Washington, DC. 167 pp.

Lee, G.F., E. Bentley, and R. Amundson. 1975. Effects of marshes on water quality. *In*: A.D. Hasler (editor). Coupling of Land and Water Systems. Springer-Verlag, New York, NY. pp. 105-127.

Lee, C.R., R.E. Hoeppel, P.G. Hunt, and C.A. Carlson. 1976. Feasibility of the Functional Use of Vegetation to Filter, Dewater, and Remove Contaminants from Dredged Material. Tech. Report. D-76-4. U.S. Army Engineers, Waterways Expt. Station, Vicksburg, MS.

Lieth, H. 1975. Primary productivity of the major vegetation units of the world. *In*: H. Lieth and R.H. Whittaker (editors). Productivity of the Biosphere. Springer-Verlag, New York, NY. pp. 203-316.

Leitch, J.A. 1981. Wetland Hydrology: State-of-the-art and Annotated Bibliography. Agric. Expt. Station, North Dakota State University, Fargo, No. Dak. Res. Report. 82. 16 pp.

Leopold, L.B. and M.G. Wolman. 1957. River Channel Patterns - Braided, Meandering, and Straight. U.S. Geol. Survey Prof. Paper 282-B.

Ludden, A.P., D.L. Frink, and D.H. Johnson. 1983. Water storage capacity of natural wetland depressions in the Devils Lake Basin of North Dakota. J. Soil and Water Cons. 38(1): 45-48.

Malcolm, J. 1978. Study of Wetland Drainage in Relation to Souris River Water Quantity and Quality as It Impacts J. Clark Salyer National Wildlife Refuge. U.S. Fish and Wildlife Service. Special Report.

Malcolm, J. 1979. Relationship of Wetland Drainage to Flooding and Water Quality Problems and the Impacts on J. Clark Salyer National Wildlife Refuge. U.S. Fish and Wildlife Service. Special Report.

Martin, C.C. 1974. Delaware's Tidal Streams. Delaware DNREC, Div. Fish and Wildlife, Dover.

McCormick, J. 1970. The natural features of Tinicum Marsh, with particular emphasis on the vegetation. *In*: Two Studies of Tinicum Marsh. The Conservation Foundation, Washington, DC. pp. 1-104.

McHugh, J.L. 1966. Management of Estuarine Fishes. Amer. Fish Society, Spec. Pub. No. 3: 133-154.

Moore, M. 1981. Pineland germ yields new antibiotic. Sunday Press (September 6, 1981), Atlantic City, NJ.

Motts, W.S. and R.W. Heeley. 1973. Wetlands and ground water. *In*: J.S. Larson (editors). A Guide to Important Characteristics and

58

Values of Freshwater Wetlands in the Northeast. University of Massachusetts, Water Resources Research Center, Amherst. Pub. No. 31. pp. 5-8.

Mudroch, A. and J. Capobianco. 1978. Study of selected metals in marshes on Lake St. Clair, Ontario. Archives Hydrobiologic. 84: 87-108.

Mundorff, M.J. 1950. Floodplain Deposits of North Carolina Piedmont and Mountain Streams as a Possible Source of Ground Water Supply. N.C. Div. Mineral Res. Bull. 59.

Newton, R.B. 1981. New England Wetlands: A Primer. University of Massachusetts, Amherst. M.S. Thesis. 84 pp.

Novitski, R.P. 1978. Hydrology of the Nevin Wetland Near Madison, Wisconsin. U.S. Geological Survey, Water Resources Investigations 78-48. 25 pp.

Odum, H.A.T., K.C. Eqel, W.J. Mitsch, and J.W. Ordway. 1975. Recycling Treated Sewage Through Cypress Wetlands in Florida. University of Florida, Center for Wetlands, Gainsville. Occasional Pub. No. 1.

Peters, D.S., D.W. Ahrenholz, and T.R. Rice. 1979. Harvest and value of wetland associated fish and shellfish. In: Greeson, et al. Wetland Functions and Values: The State of Our Understanding. Amer. Water Resources Association. pp. 606-617.

Robichaud, B. and M.F. Buell. 1973. Vegetation of New Jersey: A Study of Landscape Diversity. Rutgers University Press, New Brunswick. 340 pp.

Roman, C.T. and F.C. Daiber. 1984. Aboveground and belowground primary production dynamics of two Delaware Bay tidal marshes. Bull. Torr. Bot. Club III: 34-41.

Seibert, P. 1968. Importance of natural vegetation for the protection of the banks of streams, rivers, and canals. In: Nature and Environment Series (Vol. Freshwater), Council of Europe. pp. 35-67.

Sigafoos, R.S. 1964. Botanical Evidence of Floods and Floodplain Deposition, Vegetation, and Hydrologic Phenomena. U.S. Geol. Survey Prof. Paper 485-A.

Simpson, R.L., R.E. Good, B.J. Dubinski, J.J. Pasquale, and K.R. Philip. 1983a. Fluxes of Heavy Metals in Delaware River Freshwater Tidal Wetlands. Rutgers University, Center for Coastal and Environmental Studies, New Brunswick, NJ. 79 pp.

Simpson, R.L., R.E. Good, M.A. Leck, and D.F. Whigham. 1983b. The ecology of freshwater tidal wetlands. BioScience 33(4): 255-259.

Simpson, R.L., R.E. Good, R. Walker, and B.R. Frasco. 1983c. The role of Delaware River freshwater tidal wetlands in the retention of nutrients and heavy metals. J. Environ. Qual. 12(1): 41-48.

Sloey, W.E., R.L. Spangler, and C.W. Fetter, Jr. 1978. Management of freshwater wetlands for nutrient assimilation. In: R.E. Good, D.F. Whigham, and R.L. Simpson (editors). Freshwater Wetlands: Ecological Processes and Management Potential. Academic Press, Inc., New York, NY. pp. 321-340.

Stewart, R.E. and H.A. Kantrud. 1972. Vegetation of Prairie Potholes, North Dakota, in Relation to Quality of Water and Other Environmental Factors. U.S. Geol. Survey Prof. Paper 585-D. 36 pp.

Stuber, P.J.R. 1983. User's Handbook for Wetland Values Database. U.S. Fish and Wildlife Service. W/RMMG-83/W12. 47 pp.

Sugihara, T., C. Yearsley, J.B. Durand, and N.P. Psuty. 1979. Comparison of Natural and Altered Estuarine Systems: Analysis. Rutgers University, Center for Coastal and Environmental Studies, New Brunswick, NJ. Pub. No. NJ/RU-DEP-11-9-79. 247 pp.

Teal, J. and M. Teal. 1969. Life and Death of the Salt Marsh. Audubon/Balantine Books, New York, NY. 274 pp.

Thibodeau, F.R. and B.D. Ostro. 1981. An economic analysis of wetland protection. Environ. Manage. 12: 19-30.

U.S. Army Corps of Engineers. 1976. Natural Valley Storage: A Partnership with Nature. New England Division, Waltham, MA.

U.S. Department of Commerce. 1982. 1981 Commercial Fish Harvest — Delaware.

U.S. Department of the Interior and Department of Commerce. 1982. 1980 National Survey of Fishing, Hunting and Wildlife-Associated Recreation, Fish and Wildlife Service and Bureau of Census, Washington, DC. 156 pp.

U.S. Water Resources Council. 1977. Estimated Flood Damages. Appendix B. Nationwide Analysis Report. Washington, DC.

U.S. Water Resources Council. 1978. The Nation's Water Resources 1975-2000. Vol. 1: Summary. Washington, DC. 86 pp.

Verry, E.S. and D.H. Boelter. 1979. Peatland hydrology. In: P.E. Greeson, et al. Wetland Functions and Values: The State of Our Understanding. Amer. Water Resources Association. pp. 389-402.

Wander, W. 1980. Breeding birds of southern New Jersey cedar swamps. N.J. Audubon VI(4): 51-65.

Wang, J. and R. Kernehan. 1979. Fishes of the Delaware Estuaries, a Guide to the Early Life Histories. Ecological Analysts, Inc., Towson, MD. 410 pp.

Wharton, C.H. 1970. The Southern River Swamp - A Multiple Use Environment. School of Business Administration, Georgia State University. 48 pp.

Wharton, C.H. 1978. The Natural Environments of Georgia. Georgia Dept. of Natural Resources, Atlanta. 227 pp.

Whigham, D.F. and R.L. Simpson. 1976. The potential use of freshwater tidal marshes in the management of water quality in the Delaware River. In: J. Tourbier and R.W. Pierson, Jr. (editors). Biological Control of Water Pollution. University of Pennsylvania Press. pp. 173-186.

Windom, H.L. 1977. Ability of Salt Marshes to Remove Nutrients and Heavy Metals from Dredged Material Disposal Area Effluents. Technical Rept. D-77-37. U.S. Army Engineers, Waterways Expt. Station, Vicksburg, MS.

Woodhouse, W.W., E.D. Seneca, and S.W. Broome. 1976. Propagation and Use of Spartina alterniflora for Shoreline Erosion Abatement. U.S. Army Coastal Engineering Research Center. Tech. Rept. 76-2.

Wolman, W.G. and L.B. Leopold. 1957. River Floodplains. Some Observations on Their Formation. U.S. Geol. Survey Prof. Paper 282-C.

CHAPTER 8.

Delaware Wetland Trends

Introduction

Although conservation-minded government agencies, private groups, and individuals have recognized the importance of wetlands to fish and wildlife, Delaware's wetlands have been largely viewed as natural lands best suited for conversion to other uses such as agriculture, industrial sites, and residential housing. Many of the alternative uses require the physical destruction of wetlands and the public values they naturally provide. Other uses alter the character or quality of a wetland, but do not destroy all of its natural values. For example, diking of coastal marshes along Delaware Bay to create waterfowl impoundments has disrupted their ecology and estuarine productivity, yet these wetlands still provide wildlife habitat and function as wetland in other ways. The following discussion addresses factors causing wetland changes and presents available information on the amount of wetland change in Delaware. For information on national wetland trends, the reader is referred to **Wetlands of the United States: Current Status and Recent Trends** (Tiner 1984).

Forces Changing Wetlands

Wetlands are dynamic environments subject to change by both natural processes and human actions. These forces interact to cause wetland gains and losses as well as to degrade and improve their quality. In general, the overall effect in Delaware has been a loss and degradation of wetlands. Table 18 outlines major causes of wetland loss and degradation in the state.

Natural Processes

Natural events influencing wetlands include rising sea level, natural succession, the hydrologic cycle, sedimentation, erosion, and fire. The rise in sea level of roughly 0.41 feet per century in Delaware according to Kraft and others (1976) has the potential to both increase wetland acreage by flooding low-lying uplands and decrease wetlands through permanent flooding. Local sea level rise is due to many factors, including eustatic rise in sea level, tectonic effects, water loading, and subsidence from sediment compaction (Belknap and Kraft 1977). Maurmeyer (1984) discusses coastal wetland loss due to natural events in Delaware Bay. Natural succession and fire typically change the vegetation of a

wetland, usually with no net loss or gain in wetland acreage. The hydrologic cycle represents the natural cycle of wet and dry periods over time. During dry periods, wetlands are particularly vulnerable to drainage and filling. Deposition of water-borne sediments along rivers and streams often leads to formation of new wetlands, while erosion removes wetland acreage. Thus, natural forces act in a variety of ways to create, modify, and destroy wetlands.

Table 18. Major causes of wetland loss and degradation in Delaware (adapted from Zinn and Copeland 1982; Gosselink and Baumann 1980).

Human Threats

Direct:

1. Discharges of materials (e.g., pesticides, herbicides, other pollutants, nutrient loading from domestic sewage, urban runoff, agricultural runoff, and sediments from dredging and filling, agricultural and other land development) into waters and wetlands.
2. Filling for dredged spoil and other solid waste disposal, roads and highways, and commercial, residential and industrial development.
3. Dredging and stream channelization for navigation channels, flood protection, agricultural development, coastal housing developments and pond maintenance.
4. Construction of dikes, dams, levees and seawalls for flood control, waterfowl impoundments, water supply, irrigation and storm protection.
5. Drainage for crop production, timber production and mosquito control.
6. Flooding wetlands for creating lakes, ponds, and waterfowl impoundments.

Indirect:

1. Sediment diversion by dams, deep channels and other structures.
2. Hydrologic alterations by canals, spoil banks, roads and other structures.
3. Subsidence due to extraction of ground water.

Natural Threats

1. Subsidence (including natural rise of sea level).
2. Erosion.
3. Overwash from sandy barrier beaches.
4. Hurricanes and other storms.
5. Biotic effects, e.g., muskrat and snow goose "eat-outs" and common reed invasion.

Human Actions

Human actions have a significant impact on wetlands. Unfortunately, many human activities are destructive to natural wetlands, either by converting them to agricultural or other lands or by degrading their quality. Key human impacts in Delaware include drainage for agriculture; channelization for flood control and agriculture; filling for housing, highway, industry, and sanitary landfills; dredging for navigation channels, harbors and marinas; pond and impoundment construction; timber harvest; ground-water extraction; and various forms of water pollution and waste disposal (Figure 23). A few human actions do, however, create and preserve wetlands. Construction of ponds may create additional wetlands, although natural wetlands may be destroyed in the process. Marsh creation and restoration of previously altered wetlands can also be beneficial. Federal and state fish and wildlife agencies have traditionally managed coastal wetlands in Delaware to improve their value to waterfowl. Wetland protection efforts, such as Federal and state wetland regulatory programs, serve to help maintain and enhance Delaware's wetland resources, despite mounting pressures to convert them to other uses.

Wetland Trends

Wetland changes in coastal wetlands have been well documented by Daiber and others (1976) and Hardisky and Klemas (1983). Information on palustrine wetland trends did not exist until recently. In 1984, the Service's National Wetlands Inventory (NWI) Project, with financial support from the U.S. Environmental Protection Agency, Region III, initiated a study of recent wetland changes within the 5-state Chesapeake Bay region (i.e., Delaware, Maryland, Pennsylvania, Virginia, and West Virginia). Preliminary results for Delaware are now available. Another perspective on potential wetland changes can be obtained by comparing wetland acreage summaries from NWI mapping for Delaware with hydric soil acreages from U.S.D.A. Soil Conservation Service county soil surveys. Although such comparison does have limitations due to differences in mapping techniques and resolution, it is useful for showing general trends.

Tidal Wetland Changes

In 1938, an estimated 91,672 acres of tidal wetlands existed in Delaware and by 1973, only 83,420 acres

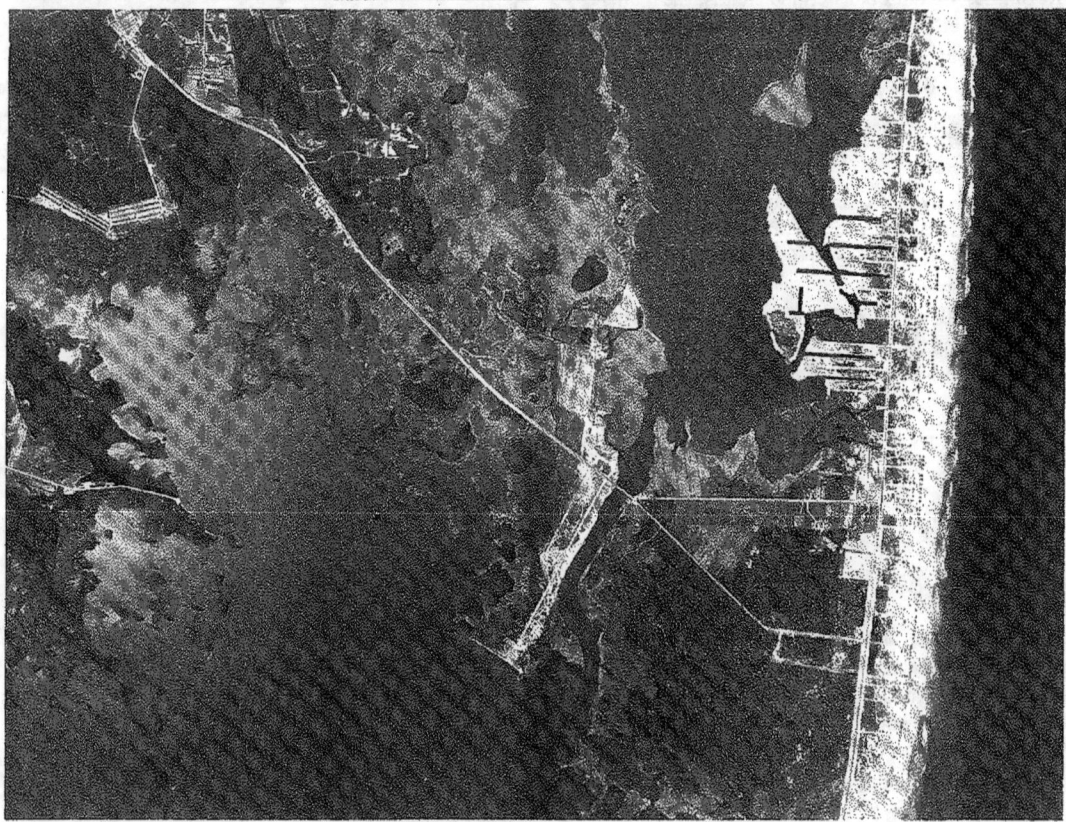

Figure 23. Human activities have had a greater impact on wetlands than natural events: (a) Fenwick Island - Bayville area in 1954 and (b) same area in 1977. Note drastic decrease in coastal wetlands along bays by dredge and fill residential developments.

remained, for a loss of 9% (Daiber, *et al.* 1976). Fifty-two percent of the loss was attributed to construction activities involving 9 acres or more, e.g., filling for housing developments, industry, and highways, with the remaining loss due to impoundments. The researchers estimated that if smaller construction projects were considered, the total loss of tidal wetlands would be 10%, with 60% of this loss due to construction activities. From 1954 to 1971, annual losses of tidal wetlands were estimated at 444 acres (Lesser 1971). The Delaware legislature enacted the Wetlands Act of 1973 to provide special protection to coastal wetlands. Wetland maps were initially prepared for regulatory purposes and in 1979 they were revised to reflect natural and human-induced changes. Hardisky and Klemas (1983) compared these maps to evaluate the magnitude and causes of any changes. They found that from 1973 to 1979 about 10 acres of coastal wetlands were lost each year to erosion, while 7 acres per year were created by natural deposition and accretion. Areas at the mouth of the Mahon River along Delaware Bay experienced shoreline erosion rates greater than 10 feet per year (D. Hardin, pers. comm.), while marsh building was active in parts of the Indian River Bay. Human activities during the study period destroyed an average of 20 acres annually. When compared with the estimated wetland loss rate of 444 acres from 1954 to 1971, a dramatic reduction in coastal wetland loss is apparent. This beneficial change has resulted from implementation of the Wetlands Act and Federal regulations under the Federal Water Pollution Control Act of 1972 (later amended to the Clean Water Act in 1977).

Palustrine Wetland Changes

Preliminary information on recent palustrine wetland trends is now available from the Service's wetland trends analysis study of the Chesapeake Bay region. This study involved analyzing wetland changes between the mid-1950's and the late 1970's/early 1980's through photo interpretation techniques. A stratified random sample of 4-square mile plots was selected within states based on land surface forms (Hammond 1970) and on known relative wetland densities. To examine trends in Delaware's freshwater wetlands, a sample of 67 plots were chosen; this sample represents about 15% of the state's inland surface area. Preliminary estimates suggest a 20% loss in palustrine vegetated wetlands (e.g., freshwater marshes and swamps) and roughly a 300% gain in ponds. The average net loss rate of

b

62

a   Zinni   b   Zinni

Figure 24. Freshwater wetlands have been drained to facilitate agricultural and other development: (a) channelized palustrine forested
wetland and   (b) farmed wetland soils adjacent to forested wetland.

palustrine vegetated wetlands may be as high as 1,500 acres per year. Most of this wetland loss was attributed to agricultural conversion, drainage by channelization projects, and forestry practices (Figure 24). Urban development of freshwater wetlands was more localized. More detailed and final results from the trends study will be presented in a special report in the near future.

A 20% loss in palustrine vegetated wetlands between the mid-1950's and the late 1970's/early 1980's is significant, but not surprising when we compare current wetland acreages from the NWI mapping with hydric soil acreage summaries from SCS's county soil surveys (Table 19). When looking at this comparison, one must keep in mind that the two surveys involved different techniques and minimum mapping units and that the SCS mapping probably had large inclusions of non-hydric soils within areas designated as a particular hydric soil. The comparison does, however, show a tremendous difference between current wetland acreage and possible pre-colonial levels for palustrine wetlands and a smaller difference for estuarine wetlands. As much as two-thirds of Delaware's original freshwater wetlands may be gone. Considering non-hydric soil inclusions within hydric soil areas, it is likely however, that the actual loss is somewhat less, perhaps in the 40-50% range. In any event, Delaware's freshwater wetlands have been significantly reduced.

Table 19. Comparison between NWI results and SCS hydric soil acreage summaries for Delaware. Note: NWI figures do not include flats, aquatic beds, open water, or beach/bars because such areas were not mapped as a soil type in SCS soil surveys.

County	Wetland Type	SCS Hydric Soils (acres)	NWI Wetlands (acres)	Change
KENT	Estuarine	38,995	39,982	+03%
	Palustrine*	147,100	46,171	−69%
	Total	186,095	86,153	−54%
NEW CASTLE	Estuarine	23,242	17,027	−27%
	Palustrine*	57,918	11,848	−80%
	Total	81,160	28,875	−64%
SUSSEX	Estuarine	26,380	22,003	−17%
	Palustrine*	186,150	71,123	−62%
	Total	212,530	93,126	−56%
STATE	Estuarine	88,617	79,012	−11%
	Palustrine*	391,168	129,142	−67%
	Total	479,785	208,154	−57%

*includes riverine tidal wetlands.

Future Outlook

Coastal wetlands appear to be well protected through implementation of the Wetlands Act of 1973 and existing Federal regulations. Future losses of these wetlands should be minimal and efforts to rehabilitate degraded wetlands may improve the status of Delaware's coastal wetlands.

The outlook for inland (nontidal) wetlands, however, is not as promising. These wetlands are not protected by state law and existing Federal regulations are not comprehensive at providing protection, i.e., they do not protect all wetlands from all human-induced activities. Federal jurisdiction regulates the deposition of fill in many wetlands, yet other human activities, e.g., excavation, normal farming practices, and silviculture are not regulated. Also, the emphasis for wetland protection is largely on water quality impacts and not fish and wildlife and other values attributed to wetlands. Eastern Sussex County, the fastest growing region in the state, is undergoing rapid development for seasonal and permanent housing (The Greeley Technical Group, Inc. 1983). Wetland development pressures are intense and expected to accelerate in the future due to projected population increases and heightened demand for real estate. Thus, future losses of inland wetlands can be expected to continue in Delaware, unless new initiatives to improve wetland protection are taken at the Federal and/or state levels. Strengthened Federal regulations, improved enforcement, and expanded state control over inland wetland uses would significantly improve the future for Delaware's inland wetlands.

References

Belknap, D.F. and J.C. Kraft. 1977. Holocene relative sea-level changes and coastal stratigraphic units on the northwest flank of the Baltimore Canyon Trough Geosyncline. J. Sed. Petrology 47: 610-629.

Daiber, F.C., L.L. Thornton, K.A. Bolster, T.G. Campbell, O.W. Crichton, G.L. Esposito, D.R. Jones, and J.M. Tyrawski. 1976. An Atlas of Delaware's Wetlands and Estuarine Resources. University of Delaware, College of Marine Studies, Newark. Delaware Coastal Mgmt. Program Tech. Rept. No. 2. 528 pp.

Gosselink, J.G. and R.H. Baumann. 1980. Wetland inventories: wetland loss along the United States coast. Z. Geomorph. N.F. Suppl. Bd. 34: 173-187.

Hammond, E.H. 1970. Physical subdivisions of the United States. *In*: National Atlas of the United States. U.S. Geological Survey, Washington, D.C. 417 pp.

Hardisky, M.A. and V. Klemas. 1983. Tidal wetlands natural and human-made changes from 1973 to 1979 in Delaware: mapping techniques and results. Environ. Manag. 7(4): 1-6.

Ireland, W., Jr. and E.D. Matthews. 1974. Soil Survey of Sussex County, Delaware. U.S.D.A. Soil Conservation Service. 74 pp. and maps.

Kraft, J.C., E.A. Allen, D.F. Belknap, C.J. John, and E.M. Maurmeyer. 1976. Delaware's Changing Shoreline. University of Delaware, Department of Geology, Newark. Delaware Coastal Zone Mgmt. Program Tech. Rept. No. 1. 319 pp.

Lesser, C.A. 1971. Memorandum to Secretary Austin N. Heller re: 1971 wetland inventory (corrected). Delaware Dept. of Natural Resources and Environmental Control, Dover. 3 pp.

Matthews, E.D. and O.L. Lavoie. 1970. Soil Survey of New Castle County, Delaware. U.S.D.A. Soil Conservation Service. 97 pp. and maps.

Matthews, E.D. and W. Ireland, Jr. 1971. Soil Survey of Kent County, Delaware. U.S.D.A. Soil Conservation Service. 66 pp. and maps.

Maurmeyer, E.M. 1984. Wetlands loss in the Delaware Bay. Paper presented at the Information Transfer Meeting of the U.S. Department of Interior, Minerals Management Service (November 1984, New Orleans, LA). 5 pp.

The Greeley Technical Group, Inc. 1983. Inland Bays Economic Study. Final Report. Prepared for the Delaware Dept. of Natural Resources and Environmental Control, Dover.

Tiner, R.W., Jr. 1984. Wetlands of the United States: Current Status and Recent Trends. U.S. Fish and Wildlife Service, National Wetlands Inventory, Washington, DC. 59 pp.

Zinn, J.A. and C. Copeland. 1982. Wetland Management. Environment and Natural Resources Policy Division, Congressional Research Service, Library of Congress. Serial No. 97-11. 149 pp.

CHAPTER 9.

Wetland Protection

Introduction

A variety of techniques are available to protect our remaining wetlands, including land-use regulations, direct acquisition, conservation easements, tax incentives, and public education. Kusler (1983) describes these techniques in great detail in **Our National Wetland Heritage - A Protection Guidebook.** Opportunities also exist for private initiatives by individual landowners, groups, and corporations to help in conserving our Nation's wetlands. Private options for land preservation are reviewed by Rusmore and others (1982).

Wetland Regulation

Several Federal and state laws regulate certain uses of many Delaware wetlands. The more significant ones include the River and Harbor Act of 1899 and the Clean Water Act of 1977 at the Federal level and the Wetlands Act of 1973 at the state level. In addition, Executive Order 11990 - "Protection of Wetlands" - requires Federal agencies to develop guidelines to minimize destruction and degradation of wetlands and to preserve and enhance wetland values. Key points of those laws are outlined in Table 20.

The foundation of Federal wetland regulation is Section 10 of the River and Harbor Act and Section 404 of the Clean Water Act. Federal permits for many types of construction in wetlands are required from the U.S. Army Corps of Engineers, but normal agricultural and silvicultural activities are exempt from permit requirements. The Service plays an active role in the permit process by reviewing permit applications and making recommendations based on environmental considerations, under authority of the Fish and Wildlife Coordination Act. Although the Federal laws in combination apply to virtually all of Delaware's wetlands, the U.S. Army Corps of Engineers' 1982 regulations for Section 404 of the Clean Water Act reduced its effectiveness for protecting wetlands. In particular, the widespread use of "nationwide permits" and the lack of strong enforcement were major weak points. Under the nationwide permit system, there was no required reporting or monitoring system, consequently there was no record of wetland loss and no effort to promote

Table 20. Summary of primary Federal and state laws relating to wetland protection in Delaware.

Name of Law	Administering Agency	Types of Wetlands Regulated	Regulated Activities
River and Harbor Act of 1899 (Section 10)	U.S. Army Corps of Engineers	Tidal wetlands below the mean high water mark; nontidal wetlands below the ordinary high water mark	Structures and/or work in or affecting navigable the U.S., including dredging and filling
Clean Water Act of 1977 (Section 404; formerly Federal Water Pollution Control Act of 1972)	U.S. Army Corps of Engineers under guidelines developed by the U.S. Environmental Protection Agency	Wetlands contiguous with all waters of the U.S.	Discharge of dredge or fill material
Wetlands Act of 1973	Department of Natural Resources and Environmental Control	Tidal wetlands, including banks, marshes, swamps and flats (must appear on official wetlands boundary map)	Any activities in wetlands, except exemptions

environmental or other public interest concerns. In Delaware, many wetlands lie above designated head-waters or exist in isolated basins and they were not protected under the 1982 regulations. Numerous law-suits were filed nationwide against the Corps by con-cerned environmental organizations over the 1982 regulatory changes. Under a recent out-of-court settle-ment agreement (National Wildlife Federation vs. Marsh), the Corps issued new regulations in October 1984 requiring closer Federal and state review of pro-posals to fill wetlands. Implementation of these new regulations needs to be monitored to assess their effec-tiveness of protecting wetlands.

State law has generally worked well to protect coastal wetlands. Since its passage in 1973, the Wetlands Act has reduced annual losses of tidal wetlands from about 444 acres to about 20 acres (Hardisky and Klemas 1983). Roughly half of this 20 acres was attributed to construction of waterfowl impoundments that are frequently subject to tidal flooding or flushing from upland runoff in the spring.

Recently, there has been much public concern over inland wetland losses. Approximately 130,000 acres of freshwater wetlands remain largely unprotected. Federal regulation as it exists does not adequately protect these wetlands.

Wetland Acquisition

Wetlands may also be protected by direct acquisition or conservation easements. Many wetlands are owned by public agencies or by private environmental organizations, although the majority are privately-owned.

The U.S. Fish and Wildlife Service's National Wild-life Refuge System was established to preserve and enhance important migratory bird wetlands at strategic locations across the country. Two National Wildlife Refuges (NWR) are located in Delaware: Bombay Hook NWR (13,422 acres of wetlands), and Prime Hook NWR (7,508 acres). Most of Bombay Hook's wetlands are estuarine emergent wetlands, whereas the majority of Prime Hook's wetlands are palustrine tidal emergent wetlands.

The State of Delaware possesses much wetland acreage, with about 14,000 acres of tidal wetland alone. Its wildlife management areas, state parks and state forests contain numerous wetlands, ponds, lakes, and streams. County and municipal parks may hold wet-lands in public ownership as well. Approximately 7,700 acres of wetland are owned by private conservation organizations, primarily Delaware Wildlands.

Exemptions	Comments
None specified	July 22, 1982 Regulations; U.S. Fish and Wildlife Service and state wildlife agency review permit applications for environmental impacts by authority of Fish and Wildlife Coordination Act.
Normal farming, silviculture, and ranching activities (including minor drainage); main-tenance of existing structures; construction or maintenance of farm ponds, irrigation ditches or maintenance of irrigation ditches; construc-tion of temporary sedimentation basins; construction or maintenance of farm roads, forest roads or temporary mining roads (within certain specifications)	July 22, 1982 Regulations; U.S. Environmental Protection Agency oversight; U.S. Fish and Wildlife Service and state wildlife agency review proposed work for environ-mental impacts by authority of Fish and Wildlife Coordination Act. Permits cannot be issued without State certification that proposed discharge meets State water quality standards. Individual permits are required for specific work in many wetlands; regional permits for certain categories of activities in specified geographic areas; nationwide permits for 25 specific activities and for discharges into wetlands above headwaters or not part of surface tributary system to interstate or navigable waters of U.S. State takeover of permit program is encouraged. New regulations were issued in October 1984.
Mosquito control activities authorized by DNREC; construction of aids to navigation; duck blinds; and footbridges; placing of boundary stakes; wildlife nesting structures; grazing, haying, hunting, fishing and trapping	Regulated wetlands are mapped. Amendment passed in 1982 allows boundary changes to be made after public notice. Hearing is not required unless an objection is received.

Future Actions

In an effort to maintain and enhance remaining wetlands, many opportunities are available to both government and the private sector. Their joint efforts will determine the future course of our Nation's wetlands. Major options have been outlined below. For a more detailed discussion, the reader is referred to Kusler (1978; 1983) and Rusmore and others (1982).

Government Options:

1. Strengthen Federal, state and local wetlands protection.

2. Ensure proper implementation of existing laws and policies through adequate staffing and improved surveillance and enforcement programs.

3. Increase wetland acquisition in vulnerable areas.

4. Remove government subsidies for wetland drainage.

5. Scrutinize cost-benefit analyses and justifications for flood control projects that involve channelization of wetlands and watercourses.

6. Provide tax incentives to private landowners to encourage wetland preservation.

7. Increase support of the Water Bank and Conservation Easement Programs.

8. Increase the number of marsh creation projects, especially related to mitigation for unavoidable wetlands losses by government-sponsored water resource projects. This should include restoration of degraded or former wetlands.

9. Enhance existing wetlands through improving water quality and providing buffer zones.

10. Monitor wetland changes especially with reference to effectiveness of state and Federal wetland protection efforts and complete the National Wetlands Inventory and periodically update the Inventory in problem areas.

11. Increase public awareness of wetland values and the status of wetlands through various media and environmental education programs.

12. Conduct research to increase our knowledge of wetland values and ecology.

Private Options:

1. Rather than drain or fill wetlands, seek alternative uses (more environmentally compatible) of those areas, e.g., timber harvest (without drainage), waterfowl production, fur harvest, hay and forage, wild rice production, hunting leases, etc.

2. Donate wetlands to private or public conservation agencies for tax purposes.

3. Maintain wetlands as open space and seek appropriate tax relief.

4. Work in concert with government agencies to help educate the public on wetland values.

5. Construct ponds in upland and manage for wetland and aquatic species.

6. Purchase Federal and state duck stamps which support wetland acquisition.

Public and private cooperation is needed to secure a promising future for our remaining wetlands. In Delaware, competition for wetlands is particularly intense between developers and the agricultural community and environmental agencies and organizations. Ways have to be found to achieve economic growth, while minimizing adverse environmental impacts. This is vital to preserving wetland values for our future generations and for fish and wildlife species.

References

Hardisky, M.A. and V. Klemas. 1983. Tidal Wetlands Natural and Human-made Changes from 1973 to 1979 in Delaware: Mapping Techniques and Results. Environ. Manag. 7(4): 1-6.

Kusler, J.A. 1978. Strengthening State Wetland Regulations. U.S. Fish and Wildlife Service, Washington, DC. FWS/OBS-78/98. 147 pp.

Kusler, J.A. 1983. Our National Wetland Heritage. A Protection Guidebook. Environmental Law Institute, Washington, DC. 167 pp.

Rusmore, B., A. Swaney, and A.D. Spader (editors). 1982. Private Options: Tools and Concepts for Land Conservation. Island Press, Covelo, CA. 292 pp.

Appendix. Vascular Plants of Delaware's Wetlands.

List of vascular plants occurring in Delaware's wetlands. Scientific names conform with the **National List of Scientific Plant Names** (U.S.D.A. Soil Conservation Service 1982). Although this list is comprehensive, it is not exhaustive, yet the majority of plants occurring in wetlands are listed. The list was compiled mainly from R.R. Tatnall's **Flora of Delaware and the Eastern Shore** and from observations during NWI field studies. An asterisk (*) denotes the state's most critically rare vascular plants associated with wetlands (DNREC Office of Nature Preserves, pers. comm.) and other rare plants according to Tatnall (1946). For additional information on rare and endangered vascular plants, see Tucker, *et al.* (1979).

Scientific Name	Plant Common Name
Lycopodiaceae	
Lycopodium alopecuroides	Foxtail Clubmoss
Lycopodium clavatum	Running Clubmoss
Lycopodium inundatum	Clubmoss
Selaginellaceae	
Selaginella apoda	Spikemoss
Isoetales	
Isoetes engelmannii	Quillwort
Isoetes riparia	Quillwort
Equisetaceae	
Equisetum fluviatile	Horsetail
Ophioglossaceae	
Botrychium dissectum	Oblique Grape Fern
Osmundaceae	
Osmunda cinnamomea	Cinnamon Fern
Osmunda claytoniana	Interrupted Fern
Osmunda regalis	Royal Fern
Polypodiaceae	
Pteridium aquilinum	Bracken Fern
Onoclea sensibilis	Sensitive Fern
Woodwardia areolata	Net-veined Chain Fern
Woodwardia virginica	Virginia Chain Fern
Athyrium filix-femina	Lady Fern
Thelypteris thelypteroides	Marsh Fern
*Dryopteris bootii	Glandular Swamp Fern
*Dryopteris clintoniana	Broad Swamp Fern
Dryopteris cristata	Crested Shield Fern
Dryopteris spinulosa	Spinulose Shield Fern
Polystichum acrostichoides	Christmas Fern
Cystopteris fragilis	Lowland Brittle Fern
Pinaceae	
Pinus rigida	Pitch Pine
Pinus serotina	Pond Pine
Pinus strobus	White Pine
Pinus taeda	Loblolly Pine
Taxodium distichum	Bald Cypress
Chamaecyparis thyoides	Atlantic White Cedar
Juniperus virginiana	Red Cedar
Typhaceae	
Typha angustifolia	Narrow-leaved Cattail
Typha latifolia	Broad-leaved Cattail

Scientific Name	Plant Common Name
Sparganiaceae	
Sparganium americanum	Eastern Burreed
Sparganium eurycarpum	Giant Burreed
Potamogetonaceae	
Potamogeton amphlifolius	Pondweed
Potamogeton crispus	Curly Pondweed
Potamogeton diversifolius	Waterthread Pondweed
Potamogeton epihydrus	Ribbonleaf Pondweed
Potamogeton foliosus	Leafy Pondweed
Potamogeton natans	Floatingleaf Pondweed
Potamogeton nodosus	Longleaf Pondweed
Potamogeton obtusifolius	Bluntleaf Pondweed
Potamogeton pectinatus	Sago Pondweed
Potamogeton perfoliatus	Thorowort Pondweed
Potamogeton pulcher	Heartleaf Pondweed
Potamogeton pusillus	Baby Pondweed
Potamogeton richardsonii	Richardson Pondweed
Potamogeton robbinsii	Robbins Pondweed
*Potamogeton spirillus	Snailseed Pondweed
Potamogeton strictifolius	Narrowleaf Pondweed
Ruppia maritima	Widgeon Grass
Zannichellia palustris	Horned Pondweed
Zostera marina	Eelgrass
Najadaceae	
Najas flexilis	Bushy Pondweed
Najas gracillima	Naiad
Najas guadalupensis	Naiad
Juncaginaceae	
*Triglochin maritima	Arrow Grass
*Triglochin striata	Arrow Grass
Alismataceae	
Alisma plantago-aquatica	Common Waterplantain
Alisma subcordatum	Subcordate Waterplantain
Sagittaria calycina	Hooded Arrowhead
*Sagittaria engelmanniana	Engelmann Arrowhead
Sagittaria graminea	Grassy Arrowhead
*Sagittaria isoetiformis	Arrowhead
Sagittaria latifolia	Broadleaf Arrowhead
Sagittaria rigida	Bur Arrowhead
*Echinodorus parvulus	Burhead
Hydrocharitaceae	
Egeria densa	Waterweed

Scientific Name	Plant Common Name	Scientific Name	Plant Common Name
Elodea canadensis	Waterweed	*Cyperaceae*	
Elodea nuttallii	Waterweed	*Cyperus dentatus*	Toothleaf Flatsedge
Limnobium spongia	Frog's Bit	*Cyperus diandrus*	Low Flatsedge
Vallisneria americana	Wild Celery	*Cyperus engelmannii*	Engelmann Flatsedge
		Cyperus erythrorhizos	Redroot Cyperus
		Cyperus esculentus	Chufa
Gramineae		*Cyperus filicinus*	Nuttall's Cyperus
Puccinellia fasciculata	Alkali Grass	*Cyperus odoratus*	Fragrant Flatsedge
Puccinellia pallida	Pale Manna Grass	*Cyperus polystachyos*	Many-spiked Flatsedge
Glyceria canadensis	Rattlesnake Manna Grass	*Cyperus rivularis*	*Nutgrass*
Glyceria obtusa	Blunt Manna Grass	*Cyperus rotundus*	Nutgrass
Glyceria septentrionalis	Eastern Manna Grass	*Cyperus strigosus*	Straw-colored Cyperus
Glyceria striata	Fowl Manna Grass	*Cyperus virens*	Green Flatsedge
Poa trivialis	Meadow Grass	*Dulichium arundinaceum*	Three-way Sedge
Distichlis spicata	Spike Grass	*Eleocharis acicularis*	Slender Spikerush
Phragmites australis	Common Reed	*Eleocharis engelmannii*	Engelmann's Spikerush
Elymus riparius	Wild Rye	*Eleocharis equisetoides*	Northern Jointed Spikerush
Elymus virginicus	Wild Rye	*Eleocharis erythropoda*	Creeping Spikerush
Hordeum jubatum	Squirrel-tail Grass	*Eleocharis flavescens*	Yellow Spikerush
Hordeum pusillum	Little Barley	*Eleocharis halophila*	Salt Marsh Spikerush
Calamagrostis canadensis	Bluejoint	*Eleocharis intermedia*	Matted Spikerush
Calamagrostis cinnoides	Hairyseed Reedgrass	*Eleocharis melanocarpa*	Black-fruited Spikerush
Agrostis hyemalis	Bent Grass	*Eleocharis microcarpa*	Torrey's Spikerush
Agrostis stolonifera	Bent Grass	*Eleocharis obtusa*	Blunt Spikerush
Cinna arundinacea	Wood Reedgrass	*Eleocharis olivacea*	Spikerush
Alopecurus carolinianus	Water Foxtail	*Eleocharis parvula*	Dwarf Spikerush
Muhlenbergia torreyana	Torrey's Muhly	*Eleocharis quadrangulata*	Squarestem Spikerush
Aristida virgata	Triple-awned Grass	*Eleocharis robbinsii*	Trianglestem Spikerush
Spartina alterniflora	Smooth Cordgrass	*Eleocharis rostellata*	Beaked Spikerush
Spartina cynosuroides	Big Cordgrass	*Eleocharis smallii*	Small's Spikerush
Spartina patens	Salt Hay Grass	*Eleocharis tenuis*	Slender Spikerush
Spartina pectinata	Slough Grass	*Eleocharis tortilis*	Twisted Spikerush
Trisetum pennsylvanicum	Swamp Trisetum	*Eleocharis tricostata*	Three-ribbed Spikerush
Phalaris arundinacea	Reed Canary Grass	*Eleocharis tuberculosa*	Large Tubercled Spikerush
Leersia oryzoides	Rice Cutgrass	*Psilocarya nitens*	Bald Rush
Leersia virginica	White Grass	*Psilocarya scirpoides*	Bald Rush
Zizania aquatica	Wild Rice	*Fimbristylis autumnalis*	Slender Fimbristylis
Leptochloa fascicularis	Bearded Sprangletop	*Fimbristylis caroliniana*	Fimbristylis
Paspalum dissectum	Mudbank Paspalum	*Fimbristylis castanea*	Salt Marsh Fimbristylis
Panicum agrostoides	Panic Grass	*Fimbristylis perpusilla*	Fimbristylis
Panicum amarum	Beach Panic Grass	*Scirpus acutus*	Hardstem Bulrush
Panicum hemitomum	Maiden Cane	*Scirpus americanus*	Olney Three-square
Panicum hirstii	Hirst's Panic Grass	*Scirpus atrovirens*	Green Bulrush
Panicum longifolium	Longleaf Panicum	*Scirpus cylindricus*	Swamp Bulrush
Panicum virgatum	Switchgrass	*Scirpus cyperinus*	Woolgrass
Dichanthelium acuminatum	Pacific Panicum	*Scirpus etuberculatus*	Swamp Bulrush
Dichanthelium acuminatum		*Scirpus expansus*	Woodland Bulrush
var. *wrightianum*	Wright's Panic Grass	*Scirpus fluviatilis*	River Bulrush
Dichanthelium dichotomum	Forked Panicum	*Scirpus polyphyllus*	Leafy Bulrush
Dichanthelium scabriusculum	Velvet Panicum	*Scirpus pungens*	Common Three-square
Dichanthelium scoparium	Velvet Panicum	*Scirpus purshianus*	Weak Bulrush
Dichanthelium sphaerocarpon	Roundseed Panicum	*Scirpus robustus*	Salt Marsh Bulrush
Echinochloa walteri	Walter's Millet	*Scirpus smithii*	Bluntscale Bulrush
Setaria geniculata	Foxtail Grass	*Scirpus subterminalis*	Water Bulrush
Setaria magna	Giant Foxtail Grass	*Scirpus validus*	Soft-stemmed Bulrush
Erianthus brevibarbis	Plume Grass	*Eriophorum gracile*	Cottongrass
Erianthus giganteus	Plume Grass	*Eriophorum virginicum*	Virginia Cottongrass
Eulalia viminea		*Fuirena pumila*	Umbrella-sedge
Cenchrus tribuloides	Sandspur	*Fuirena squarrosa*	Hairy Umbrella-sedge
Amphicarpum purshii		*Rhynchospora alba*	White Beakrush
Andropogon virginicus		*Rhynchospora capitellata*	False Bog Rush
v. *abbreviatus*	Lowland Broomsedge	*Rhynchospora cephalantha*	Capitate Beakrush
Sacciolepis striata	American Cupscale	*Rhynchospora chalarocephala*	Loose-headed Beakrush
Coelorachis rugosa	Joint Grass	*Rhynchospora corniculata*	Horned Rush
Tripsacum dactyloides	Eastern Gama Grass		

Scientific Name	Plant Common Name
Rhynchospora fusca	Brown Beakrush
Rhynchospora globularis	Pinehill Beakrush
Rhynchospora glomerata	Clustered Beakrush
Rhynchospora gracilenta	Slender Beakrush
Rhynchospora inundata	Beakrush
Rhynchospora knieskernii	Knieskern's Beakrush
Rhynchospora macrostachya	Horned Rush
Rhynchospora microcephala	Small-headed Beakrush
Rhynchospora oligantha	Few-flowered Beakrush
Rhynchospora pallida	Pale Beakrush
Rhynchospora torreyana	Torrey's Beakrush
Cladium mariscoides	Twigrush
Scleria minor	Slender Nutrush
Scleria reticularis	Netted Razorsedge
Scleria triglomerata	Whip-grass
Scleria verticillata	Low Nutgrass
Carex alata	Wingseed Sedge
Carex albolutescens	Sedge
Carex atlantica	Eastern Sedge
Carex barrattii	Barratt's Sedge
Carex bromoides	Grassy Sedge
Carex bullata	Bullsedge
Carex bushii	Sedge
Carex buxbaumii	Buxbaum Sedge
Carex canescens	Silvery Sedge
Carex collinsii	Sedge
Carex comosa	Longhair Sedge
Carex crinita	Fringed Sedge
Carex debilis	Sedge
Carex echinata	Prickly Sedge
Carex emoryi	Emory Sedge
Carex exilis	Sedge
Carex gigantea	Giant Sedge
Carex granularis	Sedge
Carex gynandra	Sedge
Carex hormathodes	Sedge
Carex howei	Howe Sedge
Carex intumescens	Sedge
Carex lacustris	River Sedge
Carex laevivaginata	Wooly Sedge
Carex lanuginosa	Wooly Sedge
Carex leptalea	Bristle-stalked Sedge
Carex lupuliformis	Hoplike Sedge
Carex lupulina	Hop Sedge
Carex lurida	Lurid Sedge
Carex meadii	Mead Sedge
Carex mitchelliana	Sedge
Carex muhlenbergii	Sedge
Carex pensylvanica	Sedge
Carex polymorpha	Sedge
Carex prasina	Sedge
Carex rostrata	Beaked Sedge
Carex scabrata	Sedge
Carex seorsa	Sedge
Carex smalliana	Sedge
Carex squarrosa	Sedge
Carex stipata	Sawbeak Sedge
Carex straminea	Sedge
Carex stricta	Tussock Sedge
Carex torta	Sedge
Carex tribuloides	Bristebract Sedge
Carex trichocarpa	Slough Sedge
Carex trisperma	Threeseeded Sedge
Carex typhina	Sedge

Scientific Name	Plant Common Name
Carex venusta	Sedge
Carex vesicaria	Inflated Sedge
Carex vestita	Sedge
Carex vulpinoidea	Fox Sedge
Carex walteriana	Sedge
Araceae	
Arisaema dracontium	Jack-in-the-pulpit
Arisaema triphyllum	Jack-in-the-pulpit
Peltandra virginica	Arrow Arum
Symplocarpus foetidus	Skunk Cabbage
Acorus calamus	Sweet Flag
Orontium aquaticum	Golden Club
Lemnaceae	
Spirodela polyrhiza	Big Duckweed
Lemna minor	Duckweed
Lemna perpusilla	Duckweed
Wolffia columbiana	Watermeal
Wolffiella floridana	Eastern Wolffiella
Eriocaulaceae	
Eriocaulon compressum	Pipewort
Eriocaulon decangulare	Ten-angle Pipewort
Eriocaulon parkeri	Parker's Pipewort
Eriocaulon septangulare	Pipewort
Xyridaceae	
Xyris caroliniana	Carolina Yellow-eyed Grass
Xyris difformis	Southern Yellow-eyed Grass
Xyris smalliana	Small's Yellow-eyed Grass
Xyris torta	Twisted Yellow-eyed Grass
Commelinaceae	
Commelina virginica	Dayflower
Pontederiaceae	
Pontederia cordata	Pickerelweed
Zosterella dubia	Water Star-grass
Heteranthera reniformis	Roundleaf Mud Plantain
Juncaceae	
Juncus acuminatus	Tapertip Rush
Juncus biflorus	Turnflower Rush
Juncus bufonius	Toad Rush
Juncus caesariensis	New Jersey Rush
Juncus canadensis	Canada Rush
Juncus coriaceus	Leathery Rush
Juncus effusus	Soft Rush
Juncus elliotti	Bog Rush
Juncus gerardii	Black Grass
Juncus marginatus	Shore Rush
Juncus militaris	Bayonet Rush
Juncus nodosus	Knotted Rush
Juncus pelocarpus	Bog Rush
Juncus repens	Creeping Rush
Juncus roemerianus	Black Needlerush
Juncus scirpoides	Needlepod Rush
Liliaceae	
Narthecium americanum	Bog Asphodel
Tolfieldia racemosa	False Asphodel
Helonias bullata	Swamp Pink
Amianthium muscaetoxicum	Fly-poison

Scientific Name	Plant Common Name	Scientific Name	Plant Common Name
Zigadenus leimanthoides	Pine Barren Deathcamas	**Betulaceae**	
Veratrum viride	False Hellebore	*Carpinus caroliniana*	Ironwood
Melanthium virginicum	Bunchflower	*Betula lenta*	Sweet Birch
Allium canadense	Wild Garlic	*Betula nigra*	River Birch
Allium vineale	Field Garlic	*Alnus maritima*	Seaside Alder
Lilium canadense	Turk's Cap Lily	*Alnus serrulata*	Common Alder
Erythronium umbilicatum	Trout Lily		
Maianthemum canadense	Canada Mayflower	**Fagaceae**	
Aletris farinosa	Colic Root	*Fagus grandifolia*	Beech
Smilax hispida	Bristly Greenbriar	*Quercus bicolor*	Swamp White Oak
Smilax laurifolia	Bamboo-vine	*Quercus falcata*	Southern Red Oak
Smilax rotundifolia	Greenbriar	*Quercus lyrata*	Overcup Oak
Smilax walteri	Redberry Greenbriar	*Quercus michauxii*	Basket Oak
		Quercus nigra	Water Oak
Haemodoraceae		*Quercus palustris*	Pin Oak
Lophiola americana	Gold-crest	*Quercus phellos*	Willow Oak
Lachnanthes caroliniana	Redroot	*Quercus rubra*	Red Oak
Iridaceae		**Ulmaceae**	
Iris prismatica	Slender Blue Flag	*Ulmus americana*	American Elm
Iris pseudacorus	Yellow Flag	*Ulmus rubra*	Slippery Elm
Iris versicolor	Blue Flag		
Sisyrinchium atlanticum	Blue-eyed Grass	**Urticaceae**	
		Urtica dioica	Stinging Nettle
Orchidaceae		*Laportea canadensis*	Wood Nettle
Platanthera blephariglottis	White Fringed Orchid	*Boehmeria cylindrica*	False Nettle
Platanthera canbyi	Orchid	*Pilea pumila*	Clearweed
Platanthera ciliaris	Yellow Fringed Orchid		
Platanthera clavellata	Green Rein Orchid	**Loranthaceae**	
Platanthera cristata	Crested Fringed Orchid	*Phoradendron flavescens*	Mistletoe
Platanthera flava	Tubercled Orchid		
Platanthera grandiflora	Large Purple Fringed Orchid	**Santalaceae**	
Platanthera lacera	Ragged Fringed Orchid	*Comandra umbellata*	Bastard Toad-flax
Platanthera nivea	Snowy Orchid		
Platanthera permoena	Fringeless Purple Orchid	**Polygonaceae**	
Pogonia ophioglossoides	Rose Pogonia	*Rumex crispus*	Sour Dock
Cleistes divaricata	Small Whorled Pogonia	*Rumex verticillatus*	Swamp Dock
Calopogon tuberosus	Grass Pink	*Polygonum amphibium*	Water Smartweed
Arethusa bulbosa	Arethusa	*Polygonum arifolium*	Halberd-leaved Tearthumb
Spiranthes cernua	Nodding Ladies' Tresses	*Polygonum atlanticum*	
Spiranthes lucida	Wide-leaved Ladies' Tresses	*Polygonum hydropiper*	Common Smartweed
Spiranthes vernalis	Ladies' Tresses	*Polygonum hydropiperoides*	Mild Waterpepper
		Polygonum lapathifolium	Smartweed
Saururaceae		*Polygonum patulum*	
Saururus cernuus	Lizard's-tail	*Polygonum pensylvanicum*	Pennsylvania Smartweed
		Polygonum persicaria	Lady's-thumb
Salicaceae		*Polygonum punctatum*	Water Smartweed
Populus deltoides	Cottonwood	*Polygonum ramosissimum*	Bushy Knotweed
Populus heterophylla	Swamp Cottonwood	*Polygonum sagittatum*	Arrow-leaved Tearthumb
Salix cordata	Heart-leaved	*Polygonum setaceum*	
Salix exigua	Sand Bar Willow	*Polygonum virginianum*	Virginia Smartweed
Salix lucida	Shining Willow		
Salix nigra	Black Willow	**Chenopodiaceae**	
Salix sericea	Silky Willow	*Chenopodium ambrosioides*	Mexican Tea
		Atriplex arenaria	Seabeach Orach
Myricaceae		*Atriplex patula*	Marsh Orach
Myrica cerifera	Wax Myrtle	*Salicornia bigelovii*	Bigelow's Glasswort
Myrica heterophylla	Evergreen Bayberry	*Salicornia europaea*	Common Glasswort
Myrica pensylvanica	Northern Bayberry	*Salicornia virginica*	Perennial Glasswort
		Suaeda linearis	Sea-blite
Juglandaceae		*Suaeda maritima*	Sea-blite
Carya cordiformis	Bitternut	*Salsola kali*	Saltwort
Carya ovata	Shagbark Hickory		

Scientific Name	Plant Common Name
Amaranthaceae	
Amaranthus cannabinus	Water Hemp
*Amaranthus pumilus	
Phytolaccaceae	
Phytolacca americana	Pokeweed
Aizoaceae	
Sesuvium maritimum	Sea Purslane
Portulacaceae	
Claytonia virginica	Spring Beauty
Caryophyllaceae	
Myosoton aquaticum	Chickweed
Stellaria longifolia	Chickweed
*Stellaria uliginosa	Chickweed
Honkenya peploides	Seabeach Sandwort
Spergularia marina	Sand Spurrey
Sagina decumbens	Trailing Pearlwort
Ceratophyllaceae	
Ceratophyllum demersum	Coontail
Nymphaeaceae	
Brasenia schreberi	Water Shield
Nuphar luteum	Spatterdock
Nymphaea odorata	White Water Lily
*Nymphaea tuberosa	Water Lily
*Nelumbo lutea	American Lotus
Magnoliaceae	
Magnolia virginiana	Sweet Bay
Liriodendron tulipifera	Tulip Tree
Ranunculaceae	
Caltha palustris	Marsh Marigold
Ranunculus ambigens	Water-plantain Spearwort
Ranunculus arbortivus	Small-flowered Crowfoot
Ranunculus bulbosus	Bulbous Buttercup
Ranunculus cymbalaria	Seaside Crowfoot
*Ranunculus flabellaris	Yellow Water Crowfoot
Ranunculus laxicaulis	Spearwort
*Ranunculus longirostris	White Water Crowfoot
Ranunculus repens	Creeping Buttercup
Ranunculus sceleratus	Cursed Crowfoot
Ranunculus septentrionalis	Swamp Buttercup
Thalictrum pubescens	Tall Meadow Rue
Clematis virginiana	Virgin's Bower
Berberidaceae	
Podophyllum peltatum	May Apple
Anonaceae	
Asimina triloba	Pawpaw
Lauraceae	
*Persea borbonia	Red Bay
Sassafras albidum	Sassafras
Lindera benzoin	Spicebush
Cruciferae	
Cakile edentula	Sea Rocket
Cardamine bulbosa	Spring Cress

Scientific Name	Plant Common Name
Cardamine pensylvanica	Bitter Cress
Cardamine rotundifolia	Bitter Cress
Nasturtium officinale	Water Cress
Rorippa palustris	Water Cress
Barbarea vulgaris	Winter Cress
Capparidaceae	
Polanisia dodecandra	
Sarraceniaceae	
Sarracenia purpurea	Pitcher Plant
Droseraceae	
*Drosera filiformis	Dew-thread
Drosera intermedia	Spatulate-leaved Sundew
Drosera linearis	Slender-leaved Sundew
*Drosera rotundifolia	Round-leaved Sundew
Crassulaceae	
Penthorum sedoides	Ditch Stonecrop
Saxifragaceae	
Saxifraga pensylvanica	Swamp Saxifrage
Chrysosplenium americanum	Golden Saxifrage
Itea virginica	Virginia Sweetspire
Hamamelidaceae	
Hamamelis virginiana	Witch Hazel
Liquidambar styraciflua	Sweet Gum
Platanaceae	
Platanus occidentalis	Sycamore
Rosaceae	
*Physocarpus opulifolius	Nine-bark
*Spiraea alba	Meadowsweet
Spiraea latifolia	Meadowsweet
Spiraea tomentosa	Steeplebush
Geum laciniatum	Avens
Crataegus viridis	Hawthorn
Rubus cuneifolius	Sand Blackberry
Rubus hispidus	Running Dewberry
Agrimonia parviflora	Agrimony
Sanguisorba canadensis	American Burnet
Rosa carolina	Carolina Rose
Rosa multiflora	Rose
Rosa palustris	Swamp Rose
Prunus pensylvanica	Pin Cherry
Prunus serotina	Black Cherry
Aronia arbutifolia	Red Chokeberry
Aronia melanocarpa	Black Chokeberry
Aronia prunifolia	Purple-fruited Chokeberry
Amelanchier arborea	Shadbush
Amelanchier canadensis	Canada Serviceberry
Leguminosae	
*Desmodium canadense	Tick-trifoil
Vicia caroliniana	Vetch
*Aeschynomene virginica	Sensitive Joint Vetch
Strophostyles helveola	Beach Pea
Strophostyles umbellata	Wild Bean
Apios americana	American Potato Bean

Scientific Name	Plant Common Name	Scientific Name	Plant Common Name
Geraniaceae		*Hypericaceae*	
Geranium pusillum	Cranesbill	Hypericum adpressum	Shore St. John's-wort
		Hypericum boreale	Northern St. John's-wort
Linaceae		Hypericum canadense	Canada St. John's-wort
Linum striatum	Flax	Hypericum densiflorum	Dense St. John's-wort
		Hypericum denticulatum	Coppery St. John's-wort
Polygalaceae		*Hypericum ellipticum	Pale St. John's-wort
*Polygala cymosa	Tall Pine Barren Milkwort	Hypericum mutilum	Dwarf St. John's-wort
Polygala cruciata	Cross-leaved Milkwort	*Hypericum prolificum	Shrubby St. John's-wort
Polygala lutea	Yellow Milkwort	Hypericum punctatum	Spotted St. John's-wort
Polygala mariana	Maryland Milkwort	Triadenum virginicum	Marsh St. John's-wort
*Polygala ramosa	Low Pine Barren Milkwort	Triadenum walteri	Large Pink St. John's-wort
Polygala sanguinea	Purple Milkwort		
		Elatinaceae	
Euphorbiaceae		Elatine americana	Waterwort
Euphorbia polygonifolia	Beach Spurge		
*Euphorbia purpurea	Wolf's Milk	*Violaceae*	
		Viola blanda	Sweet White Violet
Callitrichaceae		*Viola brittoniana	Britton Violet
Callitriche deflexa	Water Starwort	Viola conspersa	American Dog Violet
Callitriche heterophylla	Larger Water Starwort	Viola cucullata	Marsh Blue Violet
Callitriche stagnalis	Green Water Starwort	Viola emarginata	Violet
		Viola lanceolata	Lance-leaved Violet
Limnanthaceae		Viola pallens	Northern Blue Violet
Floerka proserpinacoides	False Mermaid	Viola papilionacea	Common Blue Violet
		Viola primulifolia	Primrose-leaved Violet
Anacardiaceae		*Viola rotundifolia	Round-leaved Violet
Rhus copallinum	Dwarf Sumac	Viola sagittata	Arrowleaf Violet
Toxicodendron radicans	Poison Ivy		
Toxicodendron vernix	Poison Sumac	*Lythraceae*	
		Rotala ramosior	Toothcup
Aquifoliaceae		Decodon verticillatus	Water Willow
Ilex glabra	Inkberry	Lythrum lineare	Loosestrife
Ilex laevigata	Smooth Winterberry	Lythrum salicaria	Purple Loosestrife
Ilex opaca	American Holly		
Ilex verticillata	Winterberry	*Melastomataceae*	
		*Rhexia aristosa	Awned Meadow Beauty
Celastraceae		Rhexia mariana	Meadow Beauty
Euonymus americanus	Strawberry-bush	Rhexia virginica	Meadow Beauty
Staphyleaceae		*Onagraceae*	
Staphylea trifolia	Bladdernut	Ludwigia alternifolia	Seed-box
		Ludwigia hirtella	Spindle-root
Aceraceae		Ludwigia linearis	Narrowleaf Seed-box
Acer negundo	Box Elder	Ludwigia palustris	Water Purslane
Acer rubrum	Red Maple	*Ludwigia peploides	Perennial Water Primrose
Acer saccharinum	Silver Maple	Ludwigia sphaerocarpa	Spherical-fruited Seed-box
		Epilobium angustifolium	Fireweed
Balsaminaceae		Epilobium coloratum	Purpleleaf Willowherb
Impatiens capensis	Jewelweed	Oenothera fruticosa	Sundrops
Impatiens pallida	Pale Touch-me-not	Oenothera laciniata	Cut-leaved Evening Primrose
Vitaceae		*Halorrhagidaceae*	
Vitis labrusca	Northern Fox Grape	Myriophyllum brasiliensis	Brazilian Water Milfoil
Vitis rotundifolia	Southern Fox Grape	Myriophyllum heterophyllum	Variableleaf Water Milfoil
Parthenocissus quinquefolia	Virginia Creeper	Myriophyllum humile	Lowly Water Milfoil
		Myriophyllum pinnatum	Eastern Water Milfoil
Tiliaceae		*Myriophyllum verticillatum	Needleleaf Water Milfoil
Tilia americana	Basswood	Proserpinaca palustris	Marsh Mermaidweed
		Proserpinaca pectinata	Cutleaf Mermaidweed
Malvaceae			
Kosteletzkya virginica	Seaside Mallow	*Araliaceae*	
Hibiscus moscheutos	Rose Mallow	Aralia spinosa	Hercules Club

Scientific Name	Plant Common Name
Umbelliferae	
Hydrocotyle americana	Water Pennywort
Hydrocotyle ranunculoides	Floating Pennywort
Hydrocotyle umbellata	Water Pennywort
Hydrocotyle verticillata	Whorled Pennywort
Conium maculatum	Poison Hemlock
Sium suave	Water Parsnip
*Cicuta bulbifera	Water Hemlock
Cicuta maculata	Water Hemlock
Lilaeopsis chinensis	Eastern Lilaeopsis
Ptilimnium capillaceum	Mock Bishopweed
Angelica atropurpurea	Angelica
*Oxypolis canbyi	Canby's Dropwort
Oxypolis rigidior	Stiff Cowbane
Eryngium aquaticum	Eryngium
Cornaceae	
Cornus amomum	Silky Dogwood
Nyssa sylvatica	Black Gum
Clethraceae	
Clethra alnifolia	Sweet Pepperbush
Ericaceae	
Rhododendron periclymenoides	Purple Azalea
Rhododendron viscosum	Swamp Azalea
Kalmia angustifolia	Sheep Laurel
Leucothoe racemosa	Fetterbush
Lyonia ligustrina	Maleberry
Chamaedaphne calyculata	Leatherleaf
Gaylussacia baccata	Black Huckleberry
Gaylussacia dumosa	Dwarf Huckleberry
Gaylussaaia frondosa	Dangleberry
Vaccinium corymbosum	Highbush Blueberry
Vaccinium macrocarpon	Big Cranberry
Vaccinium stramineum	Deerberry
Primulaceae	
*Hottonia inflata	Featherfoil
Lysimachia ciliata	Fringed Loosestrife
Lysimachia hybrida	Loosestrife
Lysimachia terrestris	Swamp Candles
Samolus parviflorus	Water Pimpernel
*Trientalis borealis	Starflower
Anagallis arvensis	Poor Man's Weather-glass
Plumbaginaceae	
Limonium carolinianum	Sea Lavender
*Limonium nashii	Sea Lavender
Ebenaceae	
Diospyros virginiana	Persimmon
Styracaceae	
Symplocos tinctoria	Sweet Leaf
Oleaceae	
Fraxinus americana	White Ash
Fraxinus pennsylvanica	Green Ash
Fraxinus nigra	Black Ash
Gentianaceae	
Sabatia angularis	Square-stemmed Centaury
Sabatia campanulata	Marsh Pink

Scientific Name	Plant Common Name
Sabatia difformis	Marsh Pink
Sabatia dodecandra	Marsh Pink
Sabatia stellaris	Marsh Pink
*Gentiana autumnalis	Pine Barrens Gentian
Gentiana catesbaei	Sampson's Snakeroot
Gentiana saponaria	Soapwort Gentian
Gentianopsis crinita	Fringed Gentian
Bartonia paniculata	Twining Bartonia
Bartonia virginica	Bartonia
*Nymphoides aquatica	Big Floating Heart
Nymphoides cordata	Little Floating Heart
Apocynaceae	
Apocynum cannabinum	Indian Hemp Dogbane
Apocynum sibiricum	Prairie Dogbane
Asclepiadaceae	
Asclepias incarnata	Swamp Milkweed
Asclepias lanceolata	Milkweed
Asclepias rubra	Red Milkweed
Convolvulaceae	
Convolvulus sepium	Hedge Bindweed
Cuscuta gronovii	Swamp Dodder
Boraginaceae	
Myosotis laxa	Forget-me-not
*Myosotis scorpioides	True Forget-me-not
Mertensia virginica	Bluebells
*Heliotropium curassavicum	Seaside Heliotrope
Verbenaceae	
Verbena hastata	Blue Vervain
Phyla lanceolata	Frog Fruit
Labiatae	
Teucrium canadense	Germander
Scutellaria galericulata	Common Skullcap
Scutellaria integrifolia	Hyssop Skullcap
Scutellaria lateriflora	Mad-dog Skullcap
Prunella vulgaris	Self-heal
Stachys hispida	
Stachys hyssopifolia	Hyssop Hedge-nettle
*Stachys palustris	Woundwort
Stachys tenuifolia	Hedge Nettle
Pycnanthemum muticum	Mountain Mint
Pycnanthemum verticillatum	
Lycopus americanus	Water Horehound
Lycopus amplectens	Water Horehound
Lycopus europaeus	European Bugleweed
Lycopus uniflorus	One-flower Bugleweed
Lycopus virginicus	Bugleweed
Mentha aquatica	Water Mint
Mentha arvensis	Wild Mint
Mentha gentilis	
Mentha spicata	Spearmint
Solanaceae	
Solanum dulcamara	Bittersweet Nightshade
Solanum nigrum	Common Nightshade
Scrophulariaceae	
*Scrophularia lanceolata	Figwort
Gratiola aurea	Hedge Hyssop

Scientific Name	Plant Common Name
Gratiola neglecta	Hedge Hyssop
Gratiola pilosa	Hedge Hyssop
Gratiola virginiana	Hedge Hyssop
Mimulus alatus	Sharp-winged Monkeyflower
Mimulus ringens	Square-stemmed Monkeyflower
Lindernia anagallidea	Clasping False Pimpernel
Lindernia dubia	False Pimpernel
Hemianthus micranthemoides	Nuttall's Micranthemum
Limosella aquatica	Mud-wort
Limosella subulata	Mud-wort
Chelone glabra	Turtlehead
Veronica peregrina	Speedwell
Agalinis decemloba	Gerardia
Agalinis maritima	Seaside Gerardia
Agalinis purpurea	Purple Gerardia

Bignoniaceae

Campsis radicans	Trumpet Creeper

Lentibulariaceae

Utricularia biflora	Bladderwort
Utricularia cornuta	Horned Bladderwort
Utricularia fibrosa	Fiberous Bladderwort
Utricularia geminiscapa	Hidden-flower Bladderwort
Utricularia gibba	Humped Bladderwort
Utricularia inflata	Floating Bladderwort
Utricularia intermedia	Flat-leaved Bladderwort
Utricularia juncea	Rush Bladderwort
Utricularia macrorhiza	Common Bladderwort
Utricularia minor	Lesser Bladderwort
Utricularia purpurea	Purple Bladderwort
Utricularia resupinata	Lavender Bladderwort
Utricularia subulata	Zigzag Bladderwort

Acanthaceae

Justicia americana	Water Willow
Ruellia strepens	

Rubiaceae

Mitchella repens	Partridge-berry
Diodia virginiana	Buttonweed
Cephalanthus occidentalis	Buttonbush
Galium asprellum	Rough Bedstraw
Galium tinctorium	Dye Bedstraw
Oldenlandia uniflora	

Caprifoliaceae

Viburnum acerifolium	Dockmackie
Viburnum cassinoides	Withe-rod
Viburnum dentatum	Southern Arrowwood
Viburnum lentago	Nannyberry
Viburnum nudum	Possumhaw
Viburnum opulus	Highbush Cranberry
Viburnum prunifolium	Black Haw
Viburnum recognitum	Northern Arrowwood
Sambucus canadensis	Common Elderberry
Lonicera japonica	Japanese Honeysuckle

Campanulaceae

Campanula aparinoides	Marsh Bellflower

Lobeliaceae

Lobelia boykinii	Boykin's Lobelia
Lobelia canbyi	Lobelia

Scientific Name	Plant Common Name
Lobelia cardinalis	Cardinal-flower
Lobelia elongata	Lobelia
Lobelia nuttallii	Lobelia
Lobelia puberula	Downy Lobelia
Lobelia siphilitica	Great Lobelia

Compositae

Helianthus angustifolius	Swamp Sunflower
Helianthus giganteus	Giant Sunflower
Eclipta alba	Yerba-de-tajo
Rudbeckia laciniata	Cutleaf Coneflower
Helenium autumnale	Sneezeweed
Helenium flexuosum	Sneezeweed
Bidens bidentoides	Swamp Beggar-ticks
Bidens cernua	Nodding Beggar-ticks
Bidens connata	Swamp Beggar-ticks
Bidens coronata	Tickseed Sunflower
Bidens discoidea	Discoid Beggar-ticks
Bidens frondosa	Beggar-ticks
Bidens laevis	Bur Marigold
Bidens polylepis	Beggar-ticks
Coreopsis rosea	Tickseed
Iva frutescens	High-tide Bush
Ambrosia artemisifolia	Common Ragweed
Ambrosia trifida	Giant Ragweed
Xanthium strumarium	Cockebur
Tussilago farfara	Coltsfoot
Heterotheca mariana	Golden Aster
Solidago fistulosa	Pine Barren Goldenrod
Solidago nemoralis	Goldenrod
Solidago patula	Downy Goldenrod
Solidago rugosa	Wrinkled Goldenrod
Solidago sempervirens	Seaside Goldenrod
Solidago stricta	Goldenrod
Solidago uliginosa	Bog Goldenrod
Euthamia galetorum	Narrow-leaved Goldenrod
Euthamia graminifolia	Grass-leaved Goldenrod
Euthamia minor	Narrow-leaved Bushy Goldenrod
Aster concinnus	Aster
Aster lateriflorus	Calico Aster
Aster nemoralis	Bog Aster
Aster novae-angliae	New England Aster
Aster novi-belgii	New York Aster
Aster puniceus	Swamp Aster
Aster radula	Low Rough Aster
Aster solidagineus	White-topped Aster
Aster subulatus	Annual Salt Marsh Aster
Aster tenuifolius	Perennial Salt Marsh Aster
Boltonia asteroides	Boltonia
Baccharis halimifolia	Sea Myrtle
Pluchea camphorata	Camphorweed
Pluchea foetida	Marsh Fleabane
Pluchea purpuracens	Marsh Fleabane
Sclerolepis uniflora	One-flowered Sclerolepis
Eupatoriadelphus fistulosus	Joe-Pye-weed
Eupatoriadelphus purpureus	Purple Joe-Pye-weed
Eupatorium dubius	Joe-Pye-weed
Eupatorium hyssopifolium	Thoroughwort
Eupatorium leucolepis	White-bracted Thoroughwort
Eupatorium perfoliatum	Boneset
Eupatorium pilosum	Hairy Thoroughwort
Eupatorium resinosum	Pine Barrens Boneset
Eupatorium rotundifolium	Roundleaf Joe-Pye-weed
Eupatorium serotinum	Late Eupatorium

Scientific Name	Plant Common Name
Mikania scandens	Climbing Hempweed
Liatris graminifolia	Blazing Star
Vernonia noveboracensis	New York Ironweed
Cirsium muticum	Swamp Thistle
Gnaphalium obtusifolium	Cudweed
Filaginella uliginosa	Low Cudweed
Senecio aureus	Golden Ragwort
Senecio tomentosus	Woolly Ragwort
*Sonchus arvensis	Sow Thistle
Hieracium gronovii	Hawkweed

References

Tatnall, R.R. 1946. Flora of Delaware and the Eastern Shore. An Annotated List of the Ferns and Flowering Plants of the Pennisula of Delaware, Maryland and Virginia. The Society of Natural History of Delaware. 313 pp.

Tucker, A.O., N.H. Dill, C.R. Broome, C.E. Phillips, and M.J. Maciarello. 1979. Rare and Endangered Vascular Plant Species in Delaware. U.S. Fish and Wildlife Service, Newton Corner, MA. 89 pp.

U.S.D.A. Soil Conservation Service. 1982. National List of Scientific Plant Names. Vol. 1. List of Plant Names. SCS-TP-159. 416 pp.

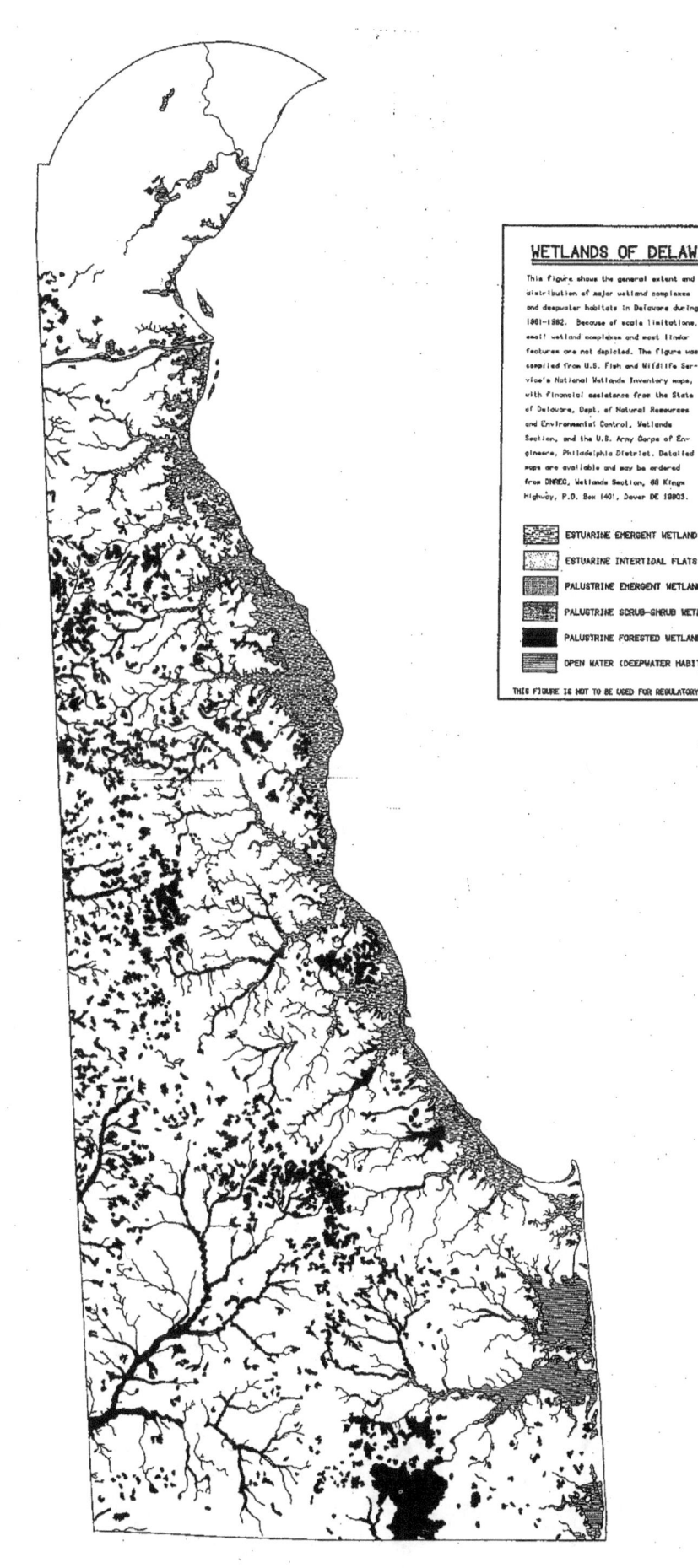

WETLANDS OF DELAWARE

This figure shows the general extent and
distribution of major wetland complexes
and deepwater habitats in Delaware during
1981-1982. Because of scale limitations,
small wetland complexes and most linear
features are not depicted. The figure was
compiled from U.S. Fish and Wildlife Service's National Wetlands Inventory maps,
with financial assistance from the State
of Delaware, Dept. of Natural Resources
and Environmental Control, Wetlands
Section, and the U.S. Army Corps of Engineers, Philadelphia District. Detailed
maps are available and may be ordered
from DNREC, Wetlands Section, 89 Kings
Highway, P.O. Box 1401, Dover DE 19903.

ESTUARINE EMERGENT WETLANDS

ESTUARINE INTERTIDAL FLATS

PALUSTRINE EMERGENT WETLANDS

PALUSTRINE SCRUB-SHRUB WETLANDS

PALUSTRINE FORESTED WETLANDS

OPEN WATER (DEEPWATER HABITATS)

THIS FIGURE IS NOT TO BE USED FOR REGULATORY PURPOSES.